MARVEL
AGE OF
COMICS

THE MIGHTY AVENGERS

VS.

THE 1970S

AN EXPLORATION BY

PAUL CORNELL

BLOOMSBURY ACADEMIC

NEW YORK • LONDON • OXFORD • NEW DELHI • SYDNEY

BLOOMSBURY ACADEMIC
Bloomsbury Publishing Inc, 1359 Broadway, New York, NY 10018, USA
Bloomsbury Publishing Plc, 50 Bedford Square, London, WC1B 3DP, UK
Bloomsbury Publishing Ireland, 29 Earlsfort Terrace, Dublin 2, D02 AY28, Ireland

BLOOMSBURY, BLOOMSBURY ACADEMIC and the Diana logo are
trademarks of Bloomsbury Publishing Plc

MARVEL PUBLISHING
Jeff Youngquist, VP, Production and Special Projects
Brian Overton, Manager, Special Projects
Sarah Singer, Editor, Special Projects
Jeremy West, Manager, Licensed Publishing
Sven Larsen, VP, Licensed Publishing
David Gabriel, VP, Print & Digital Publishing
C.B. Cebulski, Editor in Chief

BLOOMSBURY ACADEMIC
Haaris Naqvi, Global Editorial Director
Leah Babb-Rosenfeld, Editorial Director
Hali Han, Assistant Editor
Ian Buck, Deputy Head of Production
Zeba Talkhani, Senior Production Editor
Ben Anslow, Senior Designer

First published in the United States of America 2025
Reprinted 2025

© 2025 MARVEL

Cover art: Rich Buckler & John Romita Sr.
Cover design: Ben Anslow

Bloomsbury Publishing Inc does not have any control over, or responsibility for, any third-party
websites referred to or in this book. All internet addresses given in this book were correct at
the time of going to press. The author and publisher regret any inconvenience caused if
addresses have changed or sites have ceased to exist, but can accept no responsibility for any
such changes.

A catalog record for this book is available from the Library of Congress.

ISBN: PB: 979-8-7651-3180-0
           ePDF: 979-8-7651-3178-7
           eBook: 979-8-7651-3179-4

Series: Marvel Age of Comics

Typeset by RefineCatch Limited, www.refinecatch.com
Printed and bound in India

For product safety related questions contact productsafety@bloomsbury.com.

To find out more visit www.bloomsbury.com/marvel-books

CONTENTS

Introduction

This is a book about one decade in the history of the Marvel comic book *Avengers*. Specifically, it's about how that title reflected the social changes in the United States and the world across the turbulent years of the 1970s, as seen through the work of each of the title's major writers. Along the way it's a fan letter to those creators and their collaborators, all of whom I seek to treat with kindness. It's also an attempt to convey the romance, richness, and relevance that can be found in super hero comics of what's now called the Bronze Age, while not ignoring the fact that some of this material is very much of its time.

My own history with the Avengers began in September 1973, when my dad brought home for me the first issue of the British *Avengers Weekly*, reprinting #4 of the U.S. title in black and white, with some scary Doctor Strange in the back. A few months later I encountered #117 of the colourful U.S.

original in a newsagent. I was astonished by the implications about what had happened to the team in the interim. Who *were* all these new characters? And yet there was enough that was recognizable that I still felt comfortable. I think it was a desire to fill that gap in my understanding that drove my love for the title. My childhood wasn't the greatest. Amongst many psychological relics from my past is a feeling that I can never allow myself the best of anything. *Avengers*, a luxurious dessert of a book that's able to contain all the best characters and universes of Marvel, has always been an exception to that rule. And I still feel #117 is some sort of platonic ideal of a super hero comic. I simply can't be objective about it.

That lack of objectivity is also why, while I'll be using the standard model for non-fiction of referring to real people by their surnames, I won't refrain from calling comics characters by their given names.

On 5 January 1970, Richard Nixon had been the U.S. President for less than a year. B.J. Thomas was at number one in the Billboard charts with 'Raindrops Keep Fallin' on my Head.' And #74 of *Avengers* arrived on the newsstands of America. Issue #74 was not the first issue with a cover date of 1970. That was #72. But because comics were given cover dates that served to extend their life on a newsstand, #74 was the first issue of the title that one could not have picked up in 1969.

At this point, *Avengers* had been running since 1963. The

title had been a last-minute replacement when the launch of another comic, *Daredevil*, got delayed. The swift fix had been to take inspiration from Marvel's biggest competitors, the venerable DC Comics, who already had their biggest super heroes appearing together in *Justice League of America* (JLA). Marvel had done this once before, when the JLA was first created, reacting to the title's excellent sales by coming up with its own super hero team title, *Fantastic Four*, which began the Marvel Universe. *Fantastic Four* had been nothing like *JLA*, but *Avengers* was a lot closer to its DC inspiration, being first and foremost a gathering of established characters. Still, there were significant differences. To join the JLA, a character needed to already be the lead in their own comic strip, and that team was an attempt to gather *all* the heroes that rule applied to. However, the initial line-up for *Avengers* consisted of romantically-linked size-changing heroes Henry Pym and Janet Van Dyne, Ant-Man and the Wasp; armoured technocrat Tony Stark, Iron Man; Norse god of thunder Thor; and Bruce Banner, *Jekyll and Hyde* analogue the Hulk. Here were indeed a bunch of Marvel heroes with their own titles, but the Hulk had just had his cancelled, and where was mutated teen crime fighter Peter Parker, Spider-Man, who also had his own title? The Hulk left in the next issue. But then frozen super-soldier of the Second World War Steve Rogers, Captain America, also without his own title until a few months later, joined in #4.

And the revolving door had continued from there. The patchwork nature of the title – heroes with their own comics, those whose comics had been cancelled, those that might one day be promoted to a lead feature and a whole bunch that never could – was one of the continuing tensions that affected the storytelling of *Avengers* and one of the continuing joys of reading it. Here was an all-star(ish) super hero team book that was closer to messy reality than DC's equivalent. They were a quasi-official, self-appointed group of crime fighters who hung out in the very public New York venue of Tony Stark's mansion, and they were no strangers to controversy and internal conflict.

Issue #74, the first issue of the 1970s, found *Avengers* in rude health, writer Roy Thomas, supported by an excellent art team, having already enjoyed a long run on the book. The titular team at this point consisted of (renamed Ant-Man) Yellowjacket and the Wasp, who were now married; Renaissance man ruler of an African state T'Challa, the Black Panther; the emotionless android Vision; and the petulant giant Goliath, Clint Barton, who'd once been super-archer Hawkeye. (These were all characters without their own books, the pendulum having swung in that direction at this point.)

By the time of *Avengers* #193, released on 18 December 1979, there had been only three more major *Avengers* writers, and the latest of those was only just getting started. Jimmy Carter was the President and would be for two more years.

Styx were at number one in the Billboard charts with 'Babe'. And 'Earth's Mightiest Heroes' still included the Vision and the Wasp.

But so much else about the team had changed. Those changes are a window into the soul of the 1970s.

1

Roy Thomas (1970–1972)

In January 1970, current *Avengers* scripter Roy Thomas was 29 years old, and Marvel boss Stan Lee's *de facto* right-hand man. Thomas was almost two decades younger than Lee. He had started out as a comics fan and a fanzine editor. He'd come to New York in 1965 to write for Marvel's great rivals, DC Comics. He'd swiftly become disillusioned with the setup there, sought out Lee and become first a staff writer, then an editorial assistant at Marvel, his great knowledge of the company's continuity being seen as an asset. He'd joined a very small team and quickly rose to the point where Lee trusted him to write several series on his own without checking his work. In effect, Thomas had become the other editor in the building, the second 'showrunner' of the company, someone who would often be the writer to take over a title from Lee once he finished a run scripting it personally. In 1972, when Lee would be promoted to Publisher of Marvel, Thomas would thus be the obvious choice to succeed him as Editor-in-Chief. But in 1970 Thomas was still writing as many Marvel titles as he could: the villainous monarch Doctor Doom and jungle lord Ka-Zar stories in *Astonishing Tales*; blind lawyer crime fighter *Daredevil*; *Incredible Hulk*; undersea ruler Namor the *Sub-Mariner*; noble alien *Captain Marvel*; low-selling mutant students the *X-Men*; *Western Gunfighters*; and various stories in horror anthologies. Also that year he would begin his award-winning run adapting the *Conan the Barbarian* stories into comics.

But since October 1966, when he'd first co-written #35 with Lee, then taken over as solo writer with the next issue, he'd also been writing *Avengers*.

The 'Marvel Method' of scripting at the time was that a writer would plot the story, which the artist then drew, often adding a lot of plot and character, explaining their additions if required through notes on the original art. Then the writer would return to add dialog to that art, which a letterer would put on the page in speech balloons, thought bubbles and captions. Thus, some of super hero comics writing at this time was about providing the artist with a plot and some was about reacting to plotting from the artist. In one example during Thomas' run on *Avengers* from #93, in a moment not included in the script, artist Neal Adams has the tiny Ant-Man, exploring inside the android Vision's body, express surprise at something he finds, the nature of which isn't explained to the reader in that issue. Adams suggested to Thomas that what Ant-Man had discovered was that the Vision's body was originally that of the 1940s Human Torch, also canonically an android. Thomas, well-versed in the alchemy that the Marvel Method could sometimes result in, used that suggestion as the foundation for an enormous, long-running plotline. Here was someone who had learned Lee's lessons well, the proverbial safe pair of hands.

Thomas' run on *Avengers* in the 1970s includes several major story arcs: the other-dimensional warlord Arkon kidnapping mutant sorceress, and by then *Avengers* regular, Wanda, the Scarlet Witch; an attack by the vengeance-obsessed Grim Reaper and his Lethal Legion which continues the mysteries surrounding the Vision; a battle with the themed crime cartel Zodiac; an encounter with parallel world Avengers counterparts the Squadron Supreme; Thomas' masterpiece, the Kree/Skrull War, about which much more later; the Greek god Ares whipping up trouble on Earth (resulting in #100's every-Avenger team-up); and finally a battle against the mutant-hunting robot Sentinels. Between #74 and #92 most issues are drawn by John Buscema or his brother Sal. Issues #93–96 feature the photorealist art of that young DC artist Neal Adams, with #98–100 drawn by another emerging superstar,

Barry Smith. Thomas' run is completed up to #104 alongside Rich Buckler, an energetic artist with a very satisfying, very Buscema-influenced style.

Adams and Smith were outliers. The artists whose work is most associated with Thomas' run are the Buscema brothers. They're still, for me, the perfect super hero artists, their greatest panel compositions as satisfying for me as Picasso's *Violin and Grapes*. They seemingly couldn't draw anyone just standing still. There was always drama: an urgent gesture, an impassioned facial expression. Regular inker Tom Palmer (whose work provided a continuity of look across several of the artists named above) added a gloss of subtle shading to these gesticulating figures, creating an effect that looked hip and atmospheric, and still seems to this writer timeless rather than 'Seventies'. Over the page is a panel with some typically impassioned Buscema/Palmer body language.

Roy Thomas also seemed to encourage letterers to go beyond the standard Marvel style, with flourishes and different fonts abounding in his *Conan* and used to underline emotional moments in his *Avengers*, such as in #76 (by Sam Rosen) when the Scarlet Witch recalls a poem and the lettering becomes swirlingly 'poetic'.

So what was *Avengers* in 1970 like? What tropes were in place in super hero comics at the time, and how much did Roy Thomas embrace them?

Firstly, characters talk to themselves, when they're alone, out loud, all the time. For instance, in that first issue of 1970, #74, the Wasp, with nobody else present, says, 'a lot of good I'm doing the Avengers... me, the poor man's Tinker Bell!' and continues for another seven sentences of monologue. On occasion during his run, Thomas would feel the need to point out the absurdity of this behaviour, but only to give himself a pass in continuing to depict it. Thomas is only following the standard mode of super hero comics of the time, following in Stan Lee's footsteps. Who are 1970s super heroes talking to? To us, the readers, of course! Them doing so is about direct engagement with what was still at this point largely a child audience. For a modern audience to question it is like asking why the characters in a musical keep bursting into song.

Secondly, it should be noted that the emotional reactions of just about every character are continuously melodramatic – huge feelings expressed in big gestures – such as when, in #74, Yellowjacket has to restrain Goliath from kicking in the screen of the TV they're watching just because the latter is upset with something a newsreader has said. This high emotion leads to virtually unmotivated Avenger vs. Avenger fight scenes on the slightest pretext, such as when Wanda's brother Pietro, mutant speedster Quicksilver, fails to communicate his intentions to the rest of the team upon returning to them in #75. This near-continuous adolescent maelstrom is, again, because the average comics reader was still believed to be maybe about nine years old. Marvel's characters of the time yell playground emotions in an adult world, thus seeming, to those nine-year-old readers (to cite my own experience), to be *very* grown-up. One of Thomas' central talents is his ability to keep the emotional action rocketing along. And yet alongside this he manages to keep Marvel's emerging audience of college student readers engaged with genuinely mature characterization and themes, plus a clubhouse atmosphere of shared references.

Thirdly, there's the relative realism. Stan Lee had decreed from the start that Marvel's world should be one the reader recognized, with titles set in New York rather than DC's Metropolis and Gotham, and this attitude had brought with it a consideration of how ordinary people might really feel about super heroes, and thus, self-deprecating humour. Thomas returns time and again to the reactions of everyday people, a flavour of *Avengers* which persists throughout the decade. In #74, the Avengers, searching New York City, are faced with a general public that knows the precise value of their individual autographs and mocks their costumes, and a police officer who just wants them out of the way of the traffic. Issue #74 also displays Thomas' passion for social commentary. (More on that later.)

Fourthly, the comics of this time tend to make sure every action anyone takes is either explicable or explained. Our heroes don't just display their super-powers in combat, they state what they are. 'If you *were* the Black Panther,' says the Vision to an imposter in #74, 'you would never have dared leap at the Vision! You would have known that I can make my android form as ethereal as some haunted spirit—or as unyielding as the hardest diamond!' And he says all that in the brief moment when the person he's addressing is bouncing off his chest. To some extent, this is because another of Stan Lee's rules was that every issue was someone's first, and said new buyer should be given all the information required to catch up. But Thomas takes that rule a step further and answers questions about the action of the comic that most modern readers would never consider asking. Perhaps that's because Thomas' generation of comics fandom (and some might say this continues to the present day) often focused their critique on how 'real' (rather than 'realistic') what they were reading seemed; how much it was part of a coherent, explicable universe. Perhaps in the back of Thomas' mind is the inevitable letters page critique about why, for example, in #74, the Vision can't pull Goliath up onto the roof of a building, or why said giant can't just shrink down to regular size. ('Explain, please!' as *The Simpsons*' Comic Book Guy would have it.) Hence these characters spend valuable time *telling* us why they can't do these things. The more rules-based aspects of Thomas' storytelling sometimes recall the wonderfully childlike continuity litigation of DC's *Superman* line in the 1950s, where whole issues are devoted to the riddle of why our hero could or could not do something particularly novel.

Thomas often uses 'you forget' to cover those moments when one character looks surprised at another using a power they already know about. (Either because he wanted that surprised reaction for drama's sake or because that expression was there in the art to which he was adding dialogue.) In the real world, people are often surprised by extraordinary things they might have seen just once before, years ago. In early 1970s comics, such moments require clarification. One of the best examples is in #94, when Captain America forgets that Iron Man has powered roller skates hidden inside his boots(!).

Here's an awkward – in more ways than one – conversation between former Soviet super spy Natasha Romanoff (*sic*), the Black Widow (who has just entered Avengers Mansion by surprise), and Goliath, from #76:

One can feel in that dialogue pressure from so many directions at once, in terms of characterization, character voice, and fans looking over one's shoulder about continuity. But it's charming that Thomas also wants to wedge in a (continuity-based) joke about Clint's many aliases. In #77, Thomas feels obliged to include several panels about why foreign national T'Challa, the Black Panther, is legally able to be a teacher in the United States. In #92, Quicksilver can't abandon strict precision even to make a joke about his sister, the Scarlet Witch: 'Merely a mid-July relapse of spring fever.' Issue #98, we're told in a caption, occurs before, *or perhaps after*, *Thor* #198.

It's possible Thomas stayed on as the writer of *Avengers* for those 69 issues because the nature of the title focused it on such continuity matters. The stir of arriving and departing members, including those who had whatever was going on in their own titles to consider and mention, brought just about every corner of the growing Marvel Universe into play. *Fantastic Four* was a visit to a family home. *Avengers* was the town square.

Thomas' *Avengers* issues are full of references to other comics and media, both references included to indicate to the reader that the book in front of them is part of the Marvel Universe, and references he includes just for fun. In *Avengers* #93, for instance, he nods to the movie *Metropolis*, DC Comics, and fondly remembered publisher of horror comics EC in the same panel. Issue #83 includes a visit to real-life comics fan Tom Fagan's real-life Halloween comic-character costume parade in Rutland, Vermont, where two of the guests are Roy and Jeanie Thomas (Jeanie being a fellow Marvel writer and, at the time, Roy's wife). The couple are dressed as Spider-Man and the Invisible Woman (as they had been during their real-life visit that year) and other everyday folk are cheekily garbed in Marvel (or copyright-teasing versions of DC) heroes' outfits. Tom Fagan (1931–2008) was a journalist with an enormous comics collection and a similarly huge knowledge of the medium. His parade and parties brought countless comics creators to Rutland and they celebrated that by including him, and themselves, in comics for both Marvel and DC.

These nods and nudges to an informed readership are often

quite subtle. In #88, for instance, Iron Man reflects that a line of statues reminds him of something he's seen in a 'comic-mag' at the end of an abandoned subway tunnel, dialogue which has really gone out of its way to reference where the original Captain Marvel (owned by DC) got his powers. 'Now, while the under-20's are puzzling that one out—' says the following caption.

Thomas was also a science fiction fan, aware of the in-crowd language of SF fandom; dropping references to authors like H.P. Lovecraft, Nigel Kneale, L. Ron Hubbard, Philip K. Dick, and Arthur C. Clarke; and going so far as to employ SF *enfant terrible* Harlan Ellison to plot two *Avengers* issues for Thomas to dialogue (#88 and #101). Thomas sees Ellison as a selling point to the extent of mentioning his name on the cover. (Thomas was also involved in seeking out Conan and later *Star Wars* as properties for Marvel to adapt, and masterminded Marvel's own genre-adapting anthologies: *Worlds Unknown* and *Unknown Worlds of Science Fiction*.)

Alongside the continuity references and the dialogue that tries to inform the reader of too much, Thomas is also capable of some genuinely beautiful comics writing. He'll abandon dialogue altogether, or perhaps use a single phrase, to let the art speak for itself in a series of wonderful opening pages, often depicting a character approaching the reader.

For instance, in #80's 'The Coming of Red Wolf', artist John Buscema gives us four small panels showing a man being hunted through the city at night, leading to a big reveal of the titular character. Thomas' only words are: 'Rich man… poor man… beggar man… thief! Doctor… lawyer… Indian chief!!' On the second page of #95, Neal Adams' clear storytelling is allowed to accomplish twelve panels of silent exposition with only three small captions diagonally across the page.

Another trait that shows Thomas' willingness to trust the artist is when he'll suspend the last word of a line of dialogue to land at the end of a series of action panels, such as when 'This all seems so easy—far too—' leads to the image below.

Or the following images, where perhaps because Thomas feels the need to clarify what's going on, or because if they were silent the panels would look a little odd, he adds lots of text but still

ends the sequence on this lovely reflective moment.

Thomas also offers many examples of pleasing and witty dialogue. 'List, ye heralds of hatred and holocaust!' cries Thor in a very *Beowulf* moment in #96. 'Somewhere in that droplet universe-that infinity of fate and fluid…' muses alien enforcer Ronan the Accuser in #91. Issue #95 has a gangster splutter, 'Who, me? Hurt a kid? Not unless I got to.' And Cornelius Van Lunt, secret boss of the Zodiac cartel, has a fine line in heightened and rather knowing dialogue. 'I shall fill you in, officer…', he says in #77, 'as you have seldom been filled in before!'

Plotting story for a long-running comic is one of the toughest gigs in the business. Writers develop particular story shapes they keep coming back to. Thomas, perhaps influenced by the surprise reveals of those Golden Age comics, is a great fan of clever tricks played by our heroes. For instance, in #79, the Vision swaps places with one of the villains in an issue which pulls the rug out from under the reader several times. In #80–82, the Avengers make much drama out of separating into groups to address the issues of the Zodiac crime cartel, organized crime in general, and the societal problems the Native American hero Red Wolf has made them aware of, and – surprise – discover it's all the same plot. Masked villains and shapeshifters often deliver these reversals. The rabble-rouser on Earth during the Kree/Skrull War isn't the politician H. Warren Craddock, but an alien Skrull. In #98, another rabble-rouser isn't 'Mr. Talon' but the war god Ares. One strikingly repeated story shape this results in is the idea that the hidden bad guy turns out to be not the obvious candidate but someone who nobody suspected. So the bad guy in #77 turns out to be not arch-capitalist Van Lunt, but a henchman with a grudge.

Unfortunately, this trait combines with Thomas' desire to put real-life social issues front and center to deliver some unfortunate results. If one has drawn one's obvious bad guy from the headlines and the real villain turns out to be someone else… that can look a lot like letting the real-life bad guy off the hook. Issue #74 is the end of a storyline about the Sons of the Serpent (Marvel's version of the Klan) attempting to frame the Black Panther and fan racial tensions. Right-wing chat show host Dan Dunn and Black pundit Montague Hale have been depicted yelling at each other on TV, using up-to-the-minute references about racial hatred in the United States. And then it's revealed that the masked leaders of the Serpents… are both of them working together in order to make a profit. (And when last the Serpents appeared, in #32, written by Stan Lee, their leader turned out to be General Chen, from an 'unfriendly foreign power'.)

Issue #79 contains a full-page letter from Black reader Phillip Mallory Jones about this. He has a few positive things to say, but it's mostly an attack on the content of those issues. (In the 1970s, Marvel often, to their credit, printed negative letters.) In #80, Thomas responds, calling the letter 'often penetrating' and stating that the point of the story was his sympathy for the justice of the Black cause. However, he concentrates on defending 'the centre' of U.S. politics against Jones' assertion that the system is rotten, without addressing several of Jones' legitimate points.

It must be said, however, that Thomas gets into this sort of trouble because he has brought these issues to the fore. The Black Panther had become, by 1970, such a central character in Thomas' *Avengers* that readers in the letters pages had started to refer to the 'Big Four' rather than the 'Big Three' (those Avengers who were obviously secure in having their own titles: Captain America, Thor, and Iron Man). Thomas often has T'Challa ponder the idea that being a super hero is less important than the political cause of his race. In #87, Thomas perhaps attempts a reverse of that Sons of the Serpent reveal when T'Challa's college room-mate M'Tumba turns out to be the masked leader of technocrat Marvel villain group A.I.M. (And rather wonderfully, M'Tumba can't in the end bring himself to kill his old friend, and laughs wryly about it. 'As they say in America—ain't that a kick in the head!') A surprising number, for the 1970s, of random supporting cast members, from surgeons to helicopter pilots, happen to be Black. The Red Wolf issues of #80-81 depict Cornelius Van Lunt as a capitalist seizing Native American land with the support of the system, show gauche Anglo tourists exploring the reservation, and use Native American dialogue. In #94, we hear: 'The finger on the button: in the end, will it matter if that hand was alien -- or green -- or protestant...?' Perhaps most surprisingly for the early 1970s, in #92 we discover that Second World War veteran, and now master spy, Nick Fury visited the Japanese-American 'relocation centres' during that conflict and isn't a supporter of anti-alien politics now because of what he saw.

In the summer of 1972, Thomas, wary of associations with the Black radical group of the same name, decided that the

Black Panther should start calling himself the Black Leopard. About a month later, he reversed course and asked his successor on *Avengers* to change it back.

Thomas' evident desire to engage with feminism has similarly mixed, if well-intentioned, results. Wanda, the Scarlet Witch, is at moments in #75–76 oddly interested in the warlord Arkon, who has abducted her against her will, wistfully keeping the flower he gave her. (Although, in #84, she brushes him off much more swiftly.) Fan-favourite character Clint Barton, as either Hawkeye or Goliath, fuelled by that continuous need for melodrama, continually acts, under Thomas and subsequent writers, as a complete boor around women. Thomas undercuts these moments with captions and reactions indicating we're not supposed to think Barton's actions are okay. For example, when it becomes clear that Wanda is actually interested in the Vision, not Clint, we read: 'For once in his life, he does something right. For once in his life—he says nothing.' (Thomas has slowly brought together Wanda and the Vision over many issues, a plotline that might have been seen as controversial at the time, being not just a metaphor for, but the biggest possible example of, 'mixed marriage'.) But clearly we're supposed to think of Hawkeye as merely an idiot, not an abuser. There are moments when Thomas clearly wants to demonstrate that Wanda is powerful and undervalued. In #79, she responds to Hawkeye's sexist assertion that he's stronger than her with silence, thinking that he's bitter about the end of his last relationship and that she doesn't want to enrage him, only for him, during battle, to accidentally knock her out and get them both captured. Similarly, in #99, she yells at her brother for trying to protect her in combat.

Thomas' complex engagement with feminism is best demonstrated in #83.

The Wasp arrives at what turns out to be a meeting of established Marvel heroines Wanda, 'Inhuman' royal with controllable hair Medusa, and the Black Widow, convened by new character the Valkyrie, who says, 'Come on in… the revolution's fine!' Despite the Wasp, as an heiress always the most privileged of Avengers, calling it a 'powderpuff protest meeting', the Valkyrie narrates an origin story which would be strikingly familiar today: that she was a research assistant whose conclusions were stolen by male superiors. She accurately points out how the female Avengers are treated by the media and their colleagues and puts the three Avengers on course to attack them: 'Up against the wall, male chauvinist pigs!' It turns out she's secretly Asgardian villain the Enchantress in disguise, but her real motives are also the product of misogyny. She has bewitched the others, but Wanda has actually seen through her from the start and has been waiting for her moment to save everyone. Despite the issue being framed as a Halloween special, there's nothing ridiculous

about the 'Liberators', as they're called in the issue (with 'Lady' only added on the cover), and they show themselves to be the men's equals in battle. 'You birds finally learned your lesson about that women's lib bull!' says Hawkeye at the end. Wanda calls him a male chauvinist pig, and she and the Wasp hint the Liberators will be back. 'And so our offbeat Halloween saga ends…' says a caption, 'but the battle of the sexes goes on… and on… and on…!'

When he became Editor-in-Chief, Thomas reached out to women writers to create what was to be a line of new titles designed to appeal to a female readership: *The Cat*, *Shanna the She-Devil* and *Night Nurse*. It was the first effort on Marvel's part to recognize the idea that women super heroes should be written by women. The plan lasted only a few issues before all the titles were cancelled.

Thomas' masterpiece during his 1970s *Avengers* issues is the Kree/Skrull War (as it came to be called by readers after the fact), an arc which arguably invents the 'event' mode of super hero comics storytelling. Thomas clearly knows he's trying something big, calling it, in #93, 'The most portentous Avengers saga of all.' He takes time with his foreshadowing to consider what turns out to be the saga's central theme: the very idea of super heroes. The conclusion the story comes to is that they're the next stage of human evolution. It feels as if Thomas starting to think about forming the *Conan* prose stories into a single continuous comics serial changes his attitude toward *Avengers*. Unlike the soap opera threading of continuing plot through most *Avengers* tales, #89–97 can be read in retrospect as a coherent story, which pulls in disparate threads for several corners of the Marvel Universe. Issue #95 especially leans into the mythic, with the origin of Inhuman leader Black Bolt's rivalry with Maximus the Mad being given a gorgeously legend-like shape. Thomas starts and ends the arc with societal issues on Earth, politician H. Warren Craddock's 'Alien Activities Commission' bringing to mind McCarthyism with its list of 153 model citizens who are actually alien spies. And yet, at heart, this epic is science fiction, with the threat of a Skrull Armada being presented in those terms (with a careful reminder, for instance, that there is no sound in space). 'Order all ethercraft to momentum zero stop', says a Skrull in

#95, bringing the sort of technobabble you'd find in SF of the time to the Marvel Universe. The alien Skrulls have tried to disrupt the Avengers and the Inhumans on Earth because they're at war with another alien race, the Kree, and seek to seize the planet as the best tactical bridgehead. But behind all of it, the Kree Supreme Intelligence has a clever trick planned, leading to the biggest possible reversal. Since this is SF, this is also where Thomas' fanboy traits go into overdrive, with many, many references being dropped. Thomas first has the Avengers' occasional teenage sidekick Rick Jones recall 'fictional' comics heroes from his youth as representing a simpler time; then, when Jones' latent psychic powers are activated, Jones uses avatars of those heroes to attack the Skrulls, bringing back into Marvel continuity a whole bunch of characters unseen since the Golden Age. It's a moment that, in a wonderful way, turns Thomas' beloved continuity references into good drama. It's also enormous wish-fulfilment that might well have connected writer and readership. One's comics fandom can literally become one's super-power!

The Kree/Skrull War to me still feels exciting, both somehow too large for super hero comics and yet all about super heroes. It's a major achievement.

Finally, I'd like to mention Thomas' most charming trait: his self-awareness about his own writing habits. I choose to hear Quicksilver telling the Vision that he 'did not like the tone in your toneless voice just then' in #92 as Thomas having a joke at Quicksilver's earnestness rather than him feeling the need to fend off future lettercol critique. In #83, the best Thomas can do about a panel that shows the Vision, who can become intangible, unable to escape boiling tar is to offer the idea that the android fears his body may be destroyed *whilst* turning ethereal, leading to the lovely following caption: 'Now, while you try to decipher that—!' In #78, the Vision tells Quicksilver 'your words are superfluous' *after* the mutant has just narrated how he got there. And I'm thinking an SF fan like Thomas has his tongue firmly in his cheek in #94 when he mentions the *Fifth* Quadrant of the Andromeda Galaxy.

Issue #86 is perhaps the most Roy Thomas issue of *Avengers* ever. It has in-jokes ('It's just weird to meet some super heroes we don't end up fightin' for a change', says Hawkeye), references to the poetry of Browning (who we're immediatcly assured also existed in the alternate universe in which it's set), self-mockery ('I won't insult your intelligence, Avengers, by explaining what's happened here today', says Doctor Spectrum), social commentary about the exclusion of the other, and it even ends on a science fiction note, with the Avengers pondering how they could ever know they've arrived back on their own Earth. There's even some stylish lettering (by Shelly Leferman) along the way.

BUT ACTS---

---PERHAPS---

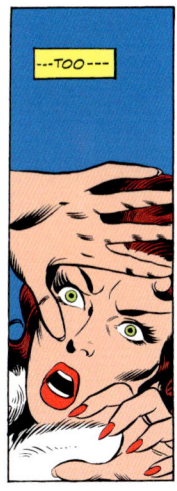

---TOO---

---LATE, AVENGERS-- BUT THAT CROSSTOWN TRAFFIC ISN'T EXACTLY--

HOLD IT! WHERE'S EVERYBODY GOING?

OUT, SHIELD-SLINGER! JARVIS JUST CLUED US IN THERE'S TROUBLE IN THE PARK ---WITH WANDA!

THE VISION'S ALREADY SCOOTED OVER THERE-- AND SO HAS PIETRO.

I JUST HOPE THEY CAN HANDLE WHATEVER- IT-IS---

"--TILL WE GET THERE!"

SZZZ ZZL

VISION-- NO! STAY BACK! HE'S ---A SENTINEL!

HE CAN ADAPT IN A MATTER OF SECONDS--- TO ANY FORCE THAT'S HURLED AGAINST HIM!

YOU CAN'T STOP HIM! NO ONE CAN!!

16.

And, as you saw on the previous page, in #102 we find perhaps the archetypal page of his storytelling, expressing almost all of his tics right at the end of his run.

In the summer of 1972, Roy Thomas took over from Stan Lee as Editor-in-Chief at Marvel, meaning he no longer had time to write so many titles. He stepped down from *Avengers*. He titled his final issue, #104, 'With a Bang—and a Whimper!'

2

Steve Englehart (1972–1976)

If Roy Thomas was the 1960s liberal *Avengers* writer, Steve Englehart was the Watergate *Avengers* writer. He was a very young U.S. Army veteran, having been honourably discharged as a Conscientious Objector to the Vietnam War. He was 23 years old when he started to work in comics, initially as an artist. He arrived at Marvel a year later, working for Thomas, first as a proof-reader and ghost writer. Then Thomas gave him a shot at a solo series, former mutant X-Man the Beast appearing in *Amazing Adventures* and turning from an erudite ape-like man into a slightly growlier furry creature.

Initially, Englehart comes over as Thomas' pupil (with Thomas continuing as editor of *Avengers* as well as being

Editor-in-Chief, a title he never actually takes on in the comic's credits). Englehart is perhaps even more interested in comics continuity, and amping up the reveals and reversals, but he seems to take the approval of lettercol hacks as a given. Despite his similar interests to Thomas, however, during his tenure the way *Avengers* stories were told was to change radically. And some of the stories he told were radical in an entirely different way.

Englehart's run features several 'events', following the example of the Kree/Skrull War, the most prominent of which is the Avengers/Defenders War. This fight between two super hero teams across both their books invents the idea that a long-form comics story could stretch across multiple comics titles. There are also three 'Kang Wars', across which this time-travelling warlord from the future becomes a major *Avengers* bad guy. But over-arching these events are two big structures: #112 to *Giant-Size Avengers* #4 is the story of Vietnamese martial arts hero Mantis (the Celestial Madonna saga); and from #137 to the end of Englehart's run in #150, he virtually re-launches the title with a bunch of new Avengers and a battle against the parallel universe hero team the Squadron Supreme. At the issue-by-issue level, defined story beginnings and endings become less important as several issues serve as connective tissue featuring many ongoing subplots. In interviews, Englehart divides his time on the title between when he was living in New York, very much one of the Marvel 'Bullpen', and his move to California from #124, which put him at mental distance from Marvel's influence, giving him the confidence to stop also writing *The Defenders* (which he loved) in order to make *Avengers* as good as it could be.

In terms of artists, Englehart had veteran Don Heck on #108–112 and George Tuska on #135–140, though there is a stint from Sal Buscema in #127–134 and Bob Brown, in #113–126, is often excellent and still under-valued. Plus there are stellar fill-ins from Rich Buckler and Jim Starlin, and Dave Cockrum on inks occasionally making things shine. But then, in #141, there arrives *the* classic Avengers artist, George Pérez, who stays until the end of Englehart's run. (Each of these art teams has fill-ins and gaps.)

As mentioned above, during Englehart's run, a new kind of *Avengers* comic appears. Marvel had experimented in 1971 with making their entire line double-sized (34 pages) and more expensive (from 15 cents to 25 cents), but had retreated from this strategy after a single issue. (#93 in the case of *Avengers*.) DC followed suit but, less nimble than Marvel, were stuck at what turned out to be an audience-shredding price point for longer, giving Marvel a considerable advantage. In 1974, Marvel tried again, but as an adjunct to the main lines rather than as a replacement. Roy Thomas returns to write *Giant-Size Avengers* #1 in 1974, which displays all his usual tics, basically stands alone, and sets up Golden Age speedster hero the Whizzer as Wanda and Pietro's father. But Englehart then uses #2–4 for major events in his ongoing arcs – even the *completion* of those arcs. The fan interest in his writing at this point is such that nobody is seen to complain in the lettercols at having to buy extra issues to discover how the stories end.

So, what sort of stories does Englehart tell?

He begins his run with a piece of continuity wrangling that would put Roy Thomas to shame. He builds #105–108 out of plot threads from *Avengers* #2, *Thor* and *Captain America*, and it all hinges around a single artistic choice from arch-stylist artist Jim Steranko in a single panel. In *Captain America* #113, page 14, panel 6 (and a caption in *Avengers* #107 tells us exactly where to look), a Steranko depiction of the villain Madame Hydra whites out her eyes, probably just to form a nice effect with the background. Englehart decides that effect depicts the moment when she's swapped out with the alien body-hopper the Space Phantom. It's a literal transformation of art into continuity. Similarly, in the final issue of Englehart's story a favourite trick of his makes its first two appearances, and it's also a form of retcon: first the Vision seems to have joined the bad guys; then the Vision says that his challenge earlier in the issue to the Phantom to turn and face him meant more than the villain imagined. On both occasions we're invited to turn back the pages and see what tiny details the artist, through directing the emphasis of the panel, made us miss the first time we read those pages: that Captain America was in the Vision's eye line, signalling him to play along, and that said challenge allowed Wanda to sneak out and save the day. There's something charmingly 'children's literature' but at the same time rather trite about being asked to flip back to see the hidden secret. (Still, this shows that Englehart was precisely directing his artists about some aspects of what he was after.) The Phantom is finally foiled using yet another continuity point, this one involving the link between Rick Jones and the alien hero Captain Marvel, and several other elements of Marvel continuity are sorted out along the way, including the Phantom making everyone forget that Cap had told the world his secret identity. Phew.

So Englehart's first story is all very finicky, but there's another level of storytelling present at the same time that's not about continuity: the Vision's experiences during the arc allow him to realize he can feel real emotion for Wanda. A new level of philosophical dialogue also starts to appear. ('But it is machine against human--momentum of planning and luck rolling over all obstacles--the tug of history--will of the gods--

humanity has many rationalizations for good falling before evil. But in cold, hard fact: sometimes being right just isn't enough.') And in #107 there's not just graffiti about using the power to vote, but an editorial caption telling us to. Something new is going on here.

Englehart's run still features characters talking out loud when they're alone, but he manages to make it feel slightly more demotic, and because he likes a clubhouse feeling with Avengers often gathered together being more friendly, they're actually alone less often. In #109, for example, Hawkeye exclaims big emotion out loud when he's alone ('I've got to get out of this Mausoleum or punch somebody!') but then his quieter thoughts are presented as thought bubbles. ('Witchie won't give me a tumble... why can't I get it on?' (It was the Seventies.)) In #121, captions describe the powers-based mechanics of the Vision rescuing Mantis from a fall rather than the two heroes telling us what's going on.

One interesting little tic of Englehart's is that when he's laid down a particularly good subtext, he can't help but also tell the reader about it. 'It is easy to see how being ridiculed as a child could make the man named Champion desire power and wealth in later years. It takes a subtler eye to note that the nine-foot-tall-man built a house which looks down upon the world', reads the caption to a picture of just such a house. And we're told, in words, that T'Challa using a one-man sky-craft says more about him that words ever could.

Englehart's dialogue and captions are chummy, fun, full of little poetic asides and ironies – like Roy Thomas but with a lot less pomp. 'This will occupy at least a chapter in my memoirs', says Kang in #129. 'Not even in your boudoirs, Halloween-nose!' replies a cop. In #140, the Beast, sneaking into a complex, tells a guard that it's okay because he's trying out for the Avengers. The guard replies he's trying out for Peter Pan in the company play. The Beast knocks him out and says, 'I hope you get the part!' As to the poetry: as our time-travelling heroes depart in #133, '1939 plays on to the empty houses of eternity forever.'

Issue #112 is one example of Englehart's conflicted, more questioning approach to writing women. Wanda is noted to be acting 'more girlish' because, she says, she's in love, but then snaps at Iron Man for assuming that her checking on the Vision's recovery when he's struck down in battle would stop her from re-joining the fray. At the end of the issue, the Black Widow, who has briefly joined the team, realizes she did so because her boyfriend Daredevil, who didn't want to join and went home, expected her to leave with him. Her independence having been demonstrated she now feels able to go back to the man she loves. In #120, we're treated to a flashback to how Stan Lee used to handle woman-vs-woman combat, with Virgo of the Zodiac crime cartel calling Wanda 'dearie' as she leaps at her. ('Dearie' is a word used so often in such fisticuffs that it had almost become Marvel code for 'catfight'.) In the following issue it's 'missie', but then Virgo knocks Wanda out with a wrench. The lettercol of #143 reveals that Englehart felt that the Vision couldn't actually father a child, despite having a human-shaped body, and, having by that point got him and the Scarlet Witch married, was going to have them adopt – until Paty Greer, who worked for Marvel in publicity and occasionally as a colourist, convinced him Wanda wouldn't want to be a mother. Here we have a super hero comics writer listening to women and adjusting his plots accordingly. In the mid-1970s, that was a quietly enormous deal.

(By 1974, Englehart had come a long way from 'dearie'.)

Issue #109 is the point where Englehart decides that said love story between the Vision and the Scarlet Witch, an arc he inherited from Thomas, will be ongoing, a central metaphor about a (literally, if not in the usual sense) mixed-race couple, with Wanda declaring to Iron Man that the Vision is 'the kindest, gentlest man in the entire blinking world'. In #110, Wanda hears from her brother Quicksilver that he's getting married to Crystal, of isolated super-powered race the Inhumans. She's happy for him and tells him about her love for the Vision, resulting – in a beautifully realistic moment – in a tirade of bigoted abuse from her brother. His hypocrisy is countered by Cap's gentle support, with some very mature writing on display. In the lettercol of #114 we hear that Englehart feels Quicksilver is bigoted, like sitcom character Archie Bunker (from *All in the Family*), because of what he perceives as prejudice against him – and in that same issue Wanda thinks Quicksilver only loves Crystal because she's 'unblemished' by contact with humans. There's a letter in #111 from Marilyn Sue Knapp that calls out Quicksilver's continual over-protectiveness of his sister as 'really strange'. This was entirely true before Englehart redefined it in terms of mutant pride. As with Hawkeye's 'brashness', it's one of those character traits that trends to the toxic when depicted in an environment where only extremely dramatic character beats are allowed. (In the 1980s this would prove the undoing of

Ant-Man/Yellowjacket/Henry Pym, whose mental breakdowns and old-fashioned marriage are destined for horrors when the only setting for them is boiling point.) 'The Vis has most of my girl friends going ga ga... Wanda can't have Vis, we want him!' says Ms. S. Otis in the lettercol of #117, noting, wisely, that marriage often means death in super hero comics. Issue #115 is a still-shocking issue where the response of the American public to news of Wanda and the Vision's android/mutant relationship varies from a Native American woman who has baked a cake for her 'soul brother' the Vision to... a group of Christian fundamentalist suicide bombers attempting to murder them. Captain America crumples up their mis-spelled hate letter, saying his God is a god of love. By the end of the issue, Wanda is left radicalized. It's an extraordinary story for the time and still shocking now.

Let's talk about an early highlight of Englehart's run.

The Avengers/Defenders War is clearly a product of Englehart finding his feet on the title, but at the same time it is a genuine epic that sticks the landing. Through the machinations of the magical cosmic dictator Dormammu and his (currently blind) henchman, the Norse god of mischief Loki, our heroes – who are looking for a way to transform former Avenger Dane Whitman, the techno-chivalric Black Knight, from stone back to flesh – are tricked into battling

This is before the word 'Holocaust' became exclusively associated with the atrocities of the Second World War.

their opposite numbers in the 'non-team' of disparate heroes the Defenders. With Englehart writing both books, this first comics crossover event seems to have been relatively easy to arrange. Individuals from each team are sent around the world to find the components of superweapon 'the Evil Eye', which the Avengers think will heal the Knight. They enter into a series of duels with their opposite numbers, arranged as chapters. The duels are, however, perhaps not as Roy Thomas would have written them – 'who would win in a fight?' as the old fanboy question has it – but instead are composed to offer maximum human drama. The exception to this is the Thor vs. Hulk battle right at the end, which is played as delicious fan service, with crowds of cheering children egging the combatants on. 'Special note from Steve and Sal: of course you can use this page for a pin-up! But, since you'll want to save the story, maybe you should buy a second copy to cut up. (No hard sell, tiger-just a friendly tip.)' It ends in a stalemate without the question of who is strongest being answered. Captain America is forced to battle his wartime compatriot the Sub-Mariner. Hawkeye, at this point with the Defenders, fights Iron Man, just as he once had back when he was a villain. And the less-developed Swordsman (another former villain, a swashbuckler who has joined the team alongside Mantis, about which more later) and Valkyrie, in the issue which I came to regard as the platonic ideal of the super hero comic, are allowed to expand on their differing forms of nobility in a fabulous fight in a castle. (The owner of the castle is portrayed as an ex-Nazi, but the lettercol of #122 reveals he was originally meant to be fleeing Watergate. Here's an early example of Englehart reining in, or having reined in, his political impulses, but perhaps it also more easily allows us to accept the moment when the Swordsman, who the castle owner has just shot, fatally runs him through.)

It's interesting that the pieces of the Evil Eye are scattered around the globe, so a different international community is visited for each duel. The results are varied in both realism and taste, but the effort shows Englehart's continually internationalist perspective. Vietnam never seems far from his thoughts in his other arcs, and he uses it as a location repeatedly and offhandedly. The two teams of heroes, of course, finally realize they've been duped and team up against the villains, who unleash chaos on Earth. The enormity of the event's finale is underlined by the presence of the cosmic chronicler the Watcher (Marvel's perennial indicator of seriousness) and by checking in on many other heroes fighting the same battle. (Readers of the time might have wondered why the conflict didn't appear in any other titles.) Finally, Wanda, the last Avenger standing, destroys the Evil

Here's one of my favourite pages from my 'perfect' issue. Such satisfying dynamic shapes!

Eye, defeating Dormammu and restoring Loki's sight but sending him mad in the process. It's a neat, logical ending that also has a mythic impact as Loki is thrown between classic archetypes: blind to mad. It's also a sign that Englehart, who'd been told by Roy Thomas when he took over *Avengers* that the Scarlet Witch should never be too powerful, wasn't satisfied with that.

At the start of Englehart's run, the Scarlet Witch had the sort of ill-defined power set which is one of the side-effects of the 'oral tradition' aspect of super hero comics, where the back-and-forth of ideas between writers, artists and letters pages still hadn't settled on anything precise in terms of what she could do. She would gesture, create a 'hex sphere' using her mutant power, in which probability went wild, then often collapse from having used too much energy. During Englehart's run he formalized what was possible for her through her mutant ability, added magical training from old witch Agatha Harkness and increased her power enormously. (In the lettercol of #132 Crystal Starkey says Agatha was the first to see Wanda as insecure and in need of support without patronizing or subjugating her. 'Don't blow it!') Wanda also went from being merely reactive to having two central character points: love for the Vision and a suspicion of humans. The arrival of George Pérez on art helped this empowerment enormously. Chris Claremont, writing *X-Men* since 1975, had put forward the radical idea that powerful women using super-powers unapologetically could delight the women reading and actually not alienate the men. (We're working from a Seventies starting point here in terms of male awareness.) Pérez's work chimes with that new paradigm, and the redefinition of the Scarlet Witch goes up another level.

In his introduction to the Marvel Masterworks volume of these issues, Englehart states that his initial idea for his defining character, Mantis – someone he'd keep coming back to for just about his entire comics career – was that she'd infiltrate the Avengers via her relationship with their disgraced former member the Swordsman, who'd previously betrayed the team, and then disrupt their ranks by creating 'sexual discord among the male Avengers'. We first meet Mantis when she saves Wanda from an attack by bigoted construction workers. She then brings the Swordsman to meet the others. The Avengers come to trust her, then help her discover that the version of her early life she remembers isn't true; that, while she really is the daughter of the Zodiac crime cartel member Libra, she was actually raised by a pacifist sect of the alien Kree, in hiding on Earth. Englehart noted in that intro that he planned that the Swordsman would nobly seek redemption while Mantis would cause the sort of dramatic disruption that Englehart's soap-style plotting thrived on. Except then (and thank goodness) Englehart discovered he liked Mantis too much. Plus he needed her to be a loyal presence on the team to make the Avengers/Defenders war work. She does indeed break up with the Swordsman, and very harshly, and comes on to the Vision, but she does so for honest reasons: she's drawn to the android's detachment, which mirrors her own perfect physical control.

The time-travelling villain Kang is at this point frequently attacking the Avengers because he knows one among their number will become 'the Celestial Madonna', and he wants to be that being's 'mate'. He assumes it can't be Mantis and thinks it's probably the Scarlet Witch. Mantis is as surprised as anyone else when *she* turns out to be the Madonna. The Swordsman flies off the handle at Mantis ditching him and Kang leaving him behind as irrelevant, and heroically sacrifices himself in battle as a super hero everyman and failure, causing Mantis to have an enormous crisis of conscience. The loop of plot that closes with the death of the Swordsman is a triumph of a finicky puzzle resolving itself into a big emotional payoff. Note in the next image the skull in the Swordsman's eye.

Next in Englehart's *Avengers* run, and continuing the 'Celestial Madonna' saga, we're treated to an extraordinary continuity-fest, as Englehart in #133–135 presents three issues in a row that are almost entirely flashbacks, a mystical journey depicting the Vision's origin story (as the robot villain Ultron's 'child', created from the body of the original Human Torch) and, in parallel, the origin of Mantis, 'including', as the caption puts it, 'the origin of the universe'. (Along the way, standoffish cosmic hero Moondragon also gets an origin!)

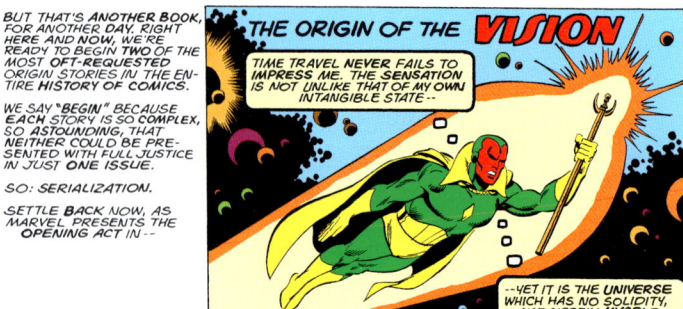

It's a peak continuity density bringing together of disparate stories, but it does so with character journeys in mind. Englehart was serious about his mysticism, going so far as to join a magic order. (His version of the Zodiac crime cartel has all members act according to their star signs.) In this journey across time, a moment is taken during the Vision's origin to reveal that he's a Virgo. But this all feels epic rather than finicky, Englehart obviously sure throughout of where all this is going. Along the way we also hit peak Seventies pop culture as it's revealed that the alien Kree created the idea of Earth martial arts: ancient astronauts were responsible for kung fu!

The Celestial Madonna storyline would surely have reminded the contemporary audience of Yoko Ono 'breaking up the Beatles'. Beatles historians now regard this racist version of events as wildly divergent from the truth, but in the 1970s this was generally accepted. Mantis, like Ono, is 'the other', an 'enigmatic' non-white foreigner whose super-powers are, according to what we hear from the audience in lettercols, over-stated. Even in current comics nostalgia podcasts you'll still hear jokes about how Englehart was obsessed with Mantis' perfection while, as the Vision says in #121 (though only to trick the villains), 'she is merely the Swordsman's girlfriend -- a hanger-on!' But time after time Englehart depicts Mantis as actually being emotionally lost in the team, pummelled by the mystery of her origins and deeply feeling her outsider status. Her powers are that strong to let her keep up with the others, and to confront the Avengers with the issue of why they won't completely accept someone so capable. Mantis is finally given official Avengers status only at the end of her arc.

Englehart very briefly engages with the Black Panther's issues early on his run, with #112 showing a confrontation between him and what look like the real-life Black Panther movement and #126 depicting a finicky continuity-based conflict with the Ambassador of 'Rudyarda', who won't shake hands with the Panther because of his skin colour but who turns out to just be the villain Klaw in disguise, all the racist intent being merely a cover story. Mostly, Englehart's engagement with racism is about how the Avengers react to Mantis. There are some problematic aspects to how she's depicted, but what becomes more and more obvious is that

Englehart is challenging the audience to accept someone who presents as 'the other' and asking at what point they'll trust her.

The end of the Celestial Madonna Saga shows Englehart at his best. A member of an alien tree race, the Cotati, animates the Swordsman's corpse and, in *Giant-Size Avengers* #4, Mantis agrees to marry him in order to bring about the birth of, we presume, the saviour. They're married alongside Wanda and the Vision, the ceremony being presided over by Immortus, a happier and wiser future version of Kang. When the Swordsman died, Kang felt unable to escape his destiny to keep attacking the Avengers. Here he is at peace and the Swordsman is (in a sense) alive. The underlying theme is very powerful: nobody is 'impure'; nobody is doomed by their past; a sex worker can still be 'the perfect woman', can still become a divine being. She at no point betrayed the team. She left the man she loved, then returned to him, in a way, making a sacrifice of her own to let everyone achieve their potential. The Vision, now seeing himself as human and capable of 'impure' love, feels able to be with Wanda. Bringing these themes together also brought together all of Englehart's ongoing stories in a wonderful fusion of theme and precision clockwork comics plotting. There's even a trademark clever trick involving the Space Phantom that's a call-back to the very start of Englehart's run.

It feels like it should have been the triumphant ending to Englehart's work on *Avengers*. Literally every plot he has set in motion is tied up in a wonderful way. But for whatever reason Englehart continued, having to start from scratch again in #137.

Englehart had never been one to shy away from political comment. 'Somebody caused a constitutional crisis on my head!' shouts returning real-life fanboy Tom Fagen in #119, and one Kang speech balloon in *Giant-Size #2* consists only of 'expletives deleted' – both Watergate references. In the pages of his run on *Captain America*, Englehart had strongly hinted that President Richard Nixon was secretly the head of the Secret Empire criminal organization, and had Cap burst into the White House to see... we don't see who... die by suicide before being caught. (Cap enters *Avengers* #125 to start telling the others about it, only to be – perhaps wisely – interrupted by everyone needing to quickly help tie-up the loose ends of Jim Starlin's Thanos/Warlock epic from the pages of *Captain Marvel*.) Issue #127 has the Inhumans' collective guilt over enslaving the Alpha Primitives manifest as a giant antagonist. Issue #130, set in Saigon – or, as Englehart refers to it, 'the land of the green latrine' – features a boorish ex-G.I. supervillain, who is 'uncaring of the tired, the poor, the huddled masses'. A Soviet super hero/villain team, The Titanic Three, are seen to dispense justice in the

Communist Zone of the country, hunting down a wife-beater. When they follow the Avengers back to an area where they have no authority, in pursuit of the G.I. super-villain, they diplomatically opt to leave him to our heroes. All the while, war hawk Iron Man has to be held back from attacking them. The requisite and deliberately meaningless battle between the teams is equated with the Vietnam War. The Titanic Three get fan mail in #130, asking for them to get a comic book of their own.

Englehart's radicalism fully expresses itself in his final *Avengers* arc. Issue #136 is a fill-in issue, a reprint from *Amazing Adventures*, the first sign of troubles to come. (Perhaps the script delay here was because of uncertainty on Englehart's part about how to begin all over again?) Issue #137 begins with an average guy getting home from work, putting on the TV and finding Thor announcing the search for new Avengers. The atmosphere feels very different to Englehart's previous issues, with a new Editor-in-Chief at Marvel, Len Wein, having replaced Englehart's mentor Roy Thomas. Englehart would later say that this was the point where others started trying to dictate his content. In the next few issues, Iron Man and Thor develop a very uncharacteristic laddish rivalry about spending time with Moondragon. The Beast, now a blue, furry, mutant acrobat, arrives as Englehart's new point-of-view character, his attempt to replace Hawkeye with someone who feels more modern for the 1970s, with his references to Stevie Wonder and Castaneda and swiftly established tendency to 'swing' with multiple beautiful women. It all feels, at the start, to be deliberately aimed at pulling the title away from the cosmic and back down to Earth. (The lettercol for #140 states the title will be concentrating on 'basic action' now.) Some of it is good fun, but some of it feels a little desperate in its relatively populist comedy. For instance, the Black Panther now had his own title, the erudite-to-the-point-of-loquacious *Jungle Action* under writer Don McGregor. When the Avengers contact the Panther to ask him about joining, here's Englehart's funny but mean translation from the genuine poetry of that series.

But from #141, under yet another new Editor-in-Chief, Marv Wolfman, Englehart hits his stride again, with the introduction of one of his own favourite characters from Marvel's past, Patsy

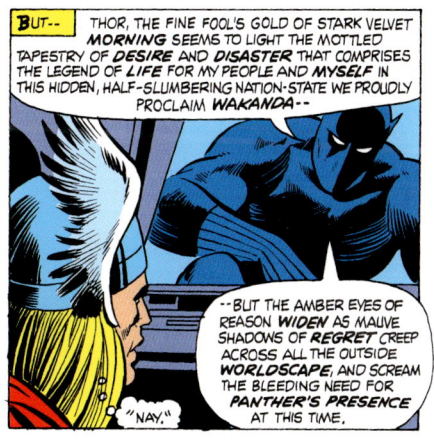

Walker; the Avengers getting involved with Marvel's cowboy heroes; and the arrival of perhaps the greatest *Avengers* artist: George Pérez.

Pérez takes the 'action figure' ethos of those issues of *Avengers* that have too many heroes packed into every panel and runs with it. He likes nothing more than too many people, too many panels, too much detail. One of his favourite tropes is something that began with super villain the Collector and artist Bob Brown in #119, our heroes trapped flat against an upright surface, arranged like figures in a box. He also loves schematics of heroes' faces down borders. When I first started reading *Avengers* as a child, I would add annotations to each panel indicating which heroes were present. Pérez's work stimulates that part of the fanboy mind, for here are heroes *arranged and listed*. But here they are also displaying a great range of 'acting', character comedy, exciting action sequences and moments of high emotion. With those two threads, continuity and character, working together, and the fact that Pérez was always seeking big dramatic moments and wasn't afraid to go beyond the script to create them, Pérez could be said to be the ideal artist for Englehart, but the artist's tropes were to influence just about every *Avengers* writer that came after, across three decades.

Englehart had read, in his youth, long runs of early Marvel's romance and western comics, and felt that the serialized soap opera plotting of the former was a great influence on his own work. He brought 'America's favourite scatterbrain' Patsy Walker from the romances, initially into his Beast strip and then into

Avengers, where she became the Hellcat, an un-liberated (she made a point of going by 'Miss') super hero who still used the vernacular of her own comic, *Patsy Walker*, which had run for twenty years until 1965. ('Cheese and crackers!') In #144, we get her life story in a flashback which includes, wonderfully, just as her own comic used to, a note that indicates 'Pat's perky print' of bikini was chosen by (supposed reader) 'Alice Hartley, NYC'. (Probably a reference to Al Hartley, long-time artist on the *Patsy Walker* comics.) Englehart was planning to take her on a journey, sending her off to study under Englehart's other newly focussed-on female character Moondragon, whose attitude of knowing her value and not deferring to men came over as considerably more 'unlikeable' then than it does now. Moondragon confronted readers and the other Avengers with (for the 1970s) unconventional beauty and uncompromising superiority. She never suffers for her arrogance, and it would have been interesting to see where Englehart would have taken the differences between her and Hellcat. As well as bringing Patsy Walker from the romance titles, in his final arc Englehart also takes the Avengers back to the western era to meet his favourite cowboy characters.

The arc resolves itself into a journey to the alternate Earth of the Squadron Supreme. Under Roy Thomas, these heroes were a fun, pretty much respectful, nod to other well-known super heroes. Englehart was to dig deeper than Thomas. His team's visit to the Squadron Supreme's alternate Earth is a powerful and passionate affair. Firstly, the Squadron aren't now the harmless take on popular super heroes they were under Thomas; they're a satire on the differences between the different comics publishers. The Golden Archer, for example, says that when the Squadron win a battle, they do so 'without any loose ends or questions'. In this world, people live in locations like Capitol City or Knickbocker City and use oaths like 'Helium and Argon!' Notably, super heroes don't rock the boat too much politically (something Captain America chides them for).

The world of the Squadron Supreme, we're told, is a world without Richard Nixon, and thus with a public naïve about corruption, and so President Nelson Rockefeller (who was the *real-life Vice-President* at this point) has been able to rise to the highest office despite being a full-on villain, using the power of the evil magical artefact the Serpent Crown to further his corrupt plans! Rockefeller turns out to be in league with the evil Brand Corporation on Marvel's main Earth, communicating across dimensions via the Crown, and we hear some stark comments on the nature of modern capitalism: 'Even a god has limits -- while a corporation doesn't!' Brand sells 'the ultimate solution' to uprisings around the world. Employed by Brand is Patsy's ex-husband, Buzz Baxter, a full-on villain in U.S. military uniform, who tells the 'dumb broad' that he 'grew up' in Vietnam while she stayed in the shallow life of romance comics. (While Englehart, immersed in romance comics, elected not to go to Vietnam.) Patsy tells him she'll scratch his eyes out, which could be a line from her old comic, only now she has super hero claws. Our heroes win the day and escape, but there's no indication the Brand Corporation or their U.S. military aides will be held to account for their crimes. The corruption continues, and a super hero battle is simply incapable of changing that underlying awfulness. Wow.

In #148, as you'll see on the next page, we get one of the most remarkable pages in all 1970s super hero comics.

That's the real-life Vice-President of the United States at the time, seemingly coming out with statements that resonate even more today. That the character is an alternate universe version, who in these panels is being impersonated by the Beast in disguise, doesn't detract from what at the time would have been an extraordinarily impactful and daring series of images. It's amazing Englehart got away with it. Or did he?

Issue #150 is the big anniversary issue, where Englehart gathers the Avengers to decide on their new membership.

But an enormous change is on the horizon.

SCENE: THE WHITE HOUSE, AT SUNDOWN...

...THE WHITE HOUSE IN CAPITOL CITY...

...WHERE EVEN A BOY FROM KNICKERBOCKER CITY CAN GROW UP TO BE PRESIDENT...

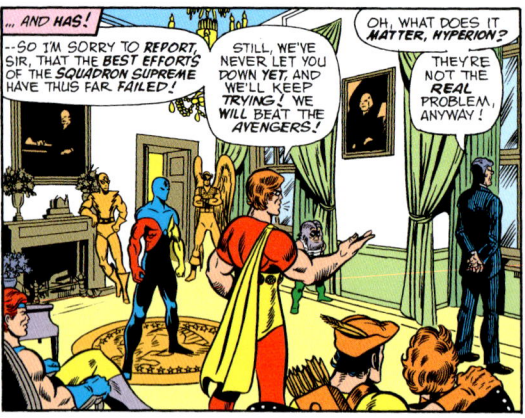

...AND HAS!

--SO I'M SORRY TO REPORT, SIR, THAT THE BEST EFFORTS OF THE SQUADRON SUPREME HAVE THUS FAR FAILED!

STILL, WE'VE NEVER LET YOU DOWN YET, AND WE'LL KEEP TRYING! WE WILL BEAT THE AVENGERS!

OH, WHAT DOES IT MATTER, HYPERION?

THEY'RE NOT THE REAL PROBLEM, ANYWAY!

I AM -- I AND ALL THE OTHER CORPORATE AND CONGLOMERATE EXECUTIVES WHO HAVE TAKEN CONTROL OF THIS COUNTRY!

WE RUN YOUR LIVES, AND YOU DON'T KNOW IT --

--SINCE SO FEW OF US EVER STEP OUT FROM BEHIND THE SCENES!

MR. PRESIDENT! WHAT ARE YOU SAYING?

EVEN THEN, ALL YOU SEE IS AN IMAGE-- A CAREFULLY-CRAFTED IMAGE, LIKE ANY OTHER PRODUCTS!

WE TALK A LOT ABOUT HONESTY, AND PRIDE, AND TEAM-SPIRIT-- BUT ALL WE REALLY WANT IS POWER!

THE TALK'S JUST TO GET YOU TO GIVE IT TO US!

AND YOU DO! WE COMMIT THE MOST OUTRAGEOUS ACTS--TURN COMPLETELY AROUND ON ANYTHING WE'VE EVER CLAIMED TO STAND FOR--

-- AND YOU GO RIGHT ALONG, PRETENDING NOT TO NOTICE!

THAT'S WHAT'S SO STRANGE! FACTS DON'T AFFECT OUR IMAGE! YOU JUST LOOK AWAY, AND WONDER WHY THE DOLLAR KEEPS LOSING ITS VALUE---

NOW JUST A MINUTE! THERE'S SOMETHING WRONG HERE!

3

A Difficult Year (1976)

Steve Englehart's run on *Avengers* had included several fill-in issues written by others and drawn by artists who weren't part of the usual team. Fill-ins were commissioned by Marvel from whoever needed the work and had the bandwidth. They were kept aside (in 'inventory') to be used in cases of what the company's cheery lexicon referred to as 'the Dreaded Deadline Doom'. The effect on the readership of having one or two issues dropped into the middle of continuing stories was alienating. Unless the editor wanted to put in a lot of extra work, the characters would suddenly stop referring to whatever ongoing soap opera they were currently involved in. Their thoughts would become generic. As a reader of the time, I recognized a fill-in immediately because it was as if my heroes had taken a step back from me.

Englehart's run had included three fill-in issues: a reprint of an *Amazing Adventures* issue in #136 (the worst sort of fill-in, when the reader might even have read the story before) and a pretty great new two-part adventure from writers Tony Isabella and Scott Edelman in #145–146 that was dropped in right after a cliff-hanger during the Serpent Crown saga. (The Beast's thoughts about death overshadowing the group served to just about set it somewhere during current continuity.) The Bullpen Bulletins (Marvel's announcements and news) page in #145 even showed what would eventually be used as #147's cover as #145's, a sign that the fill-in had had to be inserted very late, after that editorial page had gone to press. Issue #150, the big anniversary issue, under new editor Archie Goodwin, ended up as mostly a reprint of #16, with a TV news commentary awkwardly stitching the old material into the new and the issue ending with the Avengers still having not chosen their new members.

Issue #151 continues the semi-documentary approach, with visits to new super group the Champions and the Thing of the Fantastic Four for comment and the history of the Avengers being recounted, which at least lets George Pérez draw some nice tableaux. The writer credits for the issue ('a misplaced Marvel masterpiece', according to a caption), read: Gerry Conway/Jim Shooter/Steve Englehart. No editor is credited. Yellowjacket walks out on the group, then comes back by the end of the issue. Wanda gets very dramatic about whether or not her 'old buddy' Hawkeye will be a member of the team, then two pages later reacts utterly calmly to the news that he'll be on detached service with 'well, just so I know'.

The issue is very chaotic, enlivened only by visits to villains plotting future evil and a big reveal at the end of treacherous former Avenger Wonder Man still being alive. The lettercol includes an editorial signed only by 'the Bullpen' which offers an apology for the recent fill-ins. 'We're sorry that we didn't make the necessary changes before this point… Sometimes it *is* our fault. Sometimes a writer… will overcommit himself, without regard for the problems of anyone else involved.' It also states that Englehart being late with #150 had led to the chaos of the last couple of issues, and announces that Gerry Conway will be the new writer, starting next issue.

Gerry Conway had just become the latest Editor-in-Chief of Marvel Comics. Steve Englehart had just left Marvel.

Conway was 24, the successor to Stan Lee on *The Amazing Spider-Man*, responsible for some of the best-loved stories using that character. Brought into Marvel from DC by Roy Thomas, he'd established himself as able to bring interest and audience to just about any character. He was about to encounter his greatest challenge.

Conway stays writing *Avengers* for five issues (with one by Jim Shooter interrupting the run and one still following an

Englehart plot) and *Annual* #6. (The *Annuals* were from this point to take the place of the *Giant-Size* issues, their numbering felicitously continuing from both those *and* the original 1960s run of *Avengers* reprint *Annuals*.) His first issue as a plotter (#153) includes some chaotic retcons and fixes, albeit decisions made under enormous time pressure. He immediately dials down the Scarlet Witch's power back to where it was under Thomas. She's 'not a witch, not really', with Agatha Harkness stating she taught Wanda to use her mutant powers *as* witchcraft. (By #157, Conway is calling her 'a true witch' again.) She's weak enough to be shot by a random goon and, extraordinarily, she's seen flying – for the first and only time – with no explanation. (One can hear the letters pages howling. In #164, her thoughts reveal that she was testing an experimental flying belt!) Not taking on board that realistic-to-the-point-of-cynical stand-off ending of the Serpent Crown arc, he sends Wanda back to the Brand Corporation to find the Crown, which is still, incredibly, lying there in the rubble, despite its enormous value to the villains who are confirmed as still being at large and in charge. The *Annual* reveals that the army units working with Brand are 'renegades'.

The rest of Conway's run consists of an adventure in Atlantis that crosses over with *Super-Villain Team-Up* (now written by Bill Mantlo) and, while enlivened by some lovely Pérez art, it's perfectly okay super hero fare with no added dimension, nowhere near the heights Conway had reached during his great work with Spider-Man.

In #156 Jim Shooter arrives as the new permanent writer on *Avengers*.

Issue #157 is once again written by Gerry Conway.

But the next year was to begin with Conway appointee Shooter starting in earnest a run that wouldn't just steady the title but would return it to its former glories. Conway resigned from being Editor-in-Chief and went back to being a great comics writer.

It seems apt to leave 1976 with a panel from #157, the meaning of which is debatable. Here are some shop workers reacting with glee to having glimpsed their heroes. Did this play differently back in the day… or was Gerry Conway a radical too?

4

Jim Shooter (1976–1978)

In 1976, Jim Shooter was 25. He'd already been writing comics professionally for over a decade. He'd created some highly-regarded *Legion* and *Superman* stories, including the first of Superman's many races with the Flash. His first stint on staff at Marvel was at the age of 18, but he couldn't make it work financially and had to return home to Pittsburgh. He eventually started writing for DC again, but became disillusioned. Then Marvel Editor-in-Chief Marv Wolfman offered him a staff position in December 1975. Under Wolfman's successor Gerry Conway, then Conway's successor Archie Goodwin, Shooter made the best of the chaos of 1976 by being on-site and willing to do whatever needed doing. He'd already been schooled in just about every aspect of the business.

Check out Pérez's apparent enjoyment at having to draw so many heroes!

He arrived as scripter of *Avengers* with the title in chaos, steadied it, then allowed it to again reach its full potential. He did this through populism, presenting a series of straightforward stories that had well-defined beginnings and ends but which were part of a greater whole. It feels in retrospect like the 1980s arriving early. It's clearly influenced by how *Star Wars* had shaken the media landscape and made the classic forms of hero stories hip again.

Shooter is well served by his artists. He gets seven issues of Sal Buscema, seven issues of George Pérez (punctuated by equally well-regarded rising star John Byrne) and finishes his grand finale with four issues of the undervalued Dave Wenzel. Old stagers George Tuska and Don Heck are only around for an issue each. Riches indeed.

Shooter's series of stories could perhaps be described as a single story repeated four times: a man (or man-like being) gains enormous power, only to be brought down by an innate weakness connected to their flawed nature. Along the way, all the Avengers will appear to have been killed or at least defeated to the point of being scattered on the ground unconscious, with one or two of their number having first made a heroic solo stand against the enormously powerful man. Firstly, the scientist Frank Hall gains gravity powers and starts lording it over his colleagues as Graviton. Then Ultron manipulates both the Grim Reaper and Henry Pym, his Oedipus complex in full effect. Then the non-powered crime boss Count Nefaria finds a way to siphon the powers of super-villains into his own body. And finally there's Shooter's meticulously plotted masterpiece, his ten-issue uncovering of the hidden plots of cosmic entity 'The Enemy', or, as he prefers to be called, Michael.

Across these arcs, Shooter focusses on Simon Williams, Wonder Man, who had previously wandered around in a bit of a characterless daze after being brought back from the dead, and was created by Stan Lee as almost deliberately generic, a traitor who died honourably having decided to side with the Avengers. Shooter decides to develop him into feeling firstly wildly over-confident and invulnerable, then deciding to shed his costume and continue as a hero in plain clothes, while expressing a desire to pursue another career (as an actor). Simon then develops an innate fearfulness at the idea of dying again, and finally overcomes that in the climactic battle of the Shooter run. It's very satisfying character development of someone who'd previously been a non-entity. Perhaps due to the needs of marketing, or artists needing a shorthand for who they were drawing, the first 'plain clothes' look that Wonder Man opts for is one he keeps as his day, evening and all-occasion wear for years after. It consists of shades, a weirdly bulky red jacket thing that might have been high fashion for a week in the late 1970s, a black turtleneck and the sort of skin-tight trousers that Milli Vanilli would later inhabit. It looks hot in entirely the wrong sense of the word. It is also in its repetition and oddness to all intents and purposes a super hero costume.

DC's *The Legion of Super Heroes*, as the title suggests, was a book with an enormous cast of characters, and what Shooter had excelled at when writing it was giving each of them a moment to shine. He brings that to his *Avengers*, with Dave Pfeil in the lettercol of #163 noting that, in particular, having the whole team felled by a villain feels like *'Legion* storytelling'. *Avengers* is also once again the market square of the Marvel Universe, with other heroes wandering in in random encounters (like flying Defender Nighthawk attending one of the Wasp's fashion shows and the cosmically transformed powerhouse Ms. Marvel (Carol Danvers) psychically sensing trouble and flying in to help). The United States is offhandedly the centre of the action, even the place where a cosmic being like Michael decides to live to experience everyday life. The former global perspective of the title vanishes.

Shooter completely drops the idea of super heroes talking to themselves. Instead, their thought balloons are now introspective and feel like inner thoughts we're privy to as readers rather than dialogue addressed to us. Perhaps some of this is down to Marvel writer Chris Claremont, whose work on the *X-Men* was starting to make interior monologue the in-thing. The effect here, though, is startling, making *Avengers* immediately feel more modern. Also, Shooter allows characters to use everyday epithets like Wanda's 'Oh God…' in #160 rather than the picturesque oaths of previous writers. (Roy Thomas had the Vision exclaim 'In the name of the man-robot which gave me life!' and Ares say 'by the less-than-god which serve me!' Englehart had Ultron cursing 'neutrons!' and the Dread Dormammu say 'by my sister!' He also had a fine line in alien swearwords like 'calparth!' and 'quantu!' And on the alternate world of the Squadron Supreme those heroes took it to the level of 'By my mother's human heritage!') Shooter, mind you, still occasionally resorts to 'Harkov's Bones!' and 'Odin's Beard!'

One arc during Shooter's run enlarged upon a central feature of Avengers continuity: the Henry Pym/Ultron/Vision saga. During the 1960s, Roy Thomas had written the first story that saw the former Ant-Man create an intelligent robot, who escaped and forged a body for himself. Then, as was later revealed in detail under Steve Englehart, he used the android body of the original Human Torch and the thought patterns of the comatose Wonder Man to create the Vision. Thomas had also written in the 1960s the first story to indicate that Pym was unstable, with him having inhaled some mind-bending (lab) chemicals, creating the Yellowjacket identity as a brash, as-annoying-as-Hawkeye alter ego, and announcing he'd killed Henry Pym. The Wasp went along with his marriage proposal in that identity, and married him, as had always been her stated intention concerning Pym, as therapy for his condition, despite being miserable throughout.

Pym got back to normal on that occasion, but for Marvel, the home of the conflicted hero, 'normal', steadfast, science-y protagonists couldn't last. Writers of super hero comics in the 1970s always seem to have trouble with married couples. It's the end of high drama, the herald of sainted irrelevance or death.

Janet van Dyne, the Wasp, had always been fun, witty, arch. Her husband increasingly became her baggage. Thomas' script for #93 had suggested a new direction for the character: a return to the Ant-Man persona with Pym wisecracking Yellowjacket-style, albeit not as crassly, and dropping contemporary references while tiny, because a tiny hero should be fun. This was followed up on, in the end, not with Pym but with ex-con Scott Lang taking on the Ant-Man role (in *Marvel Premiere*

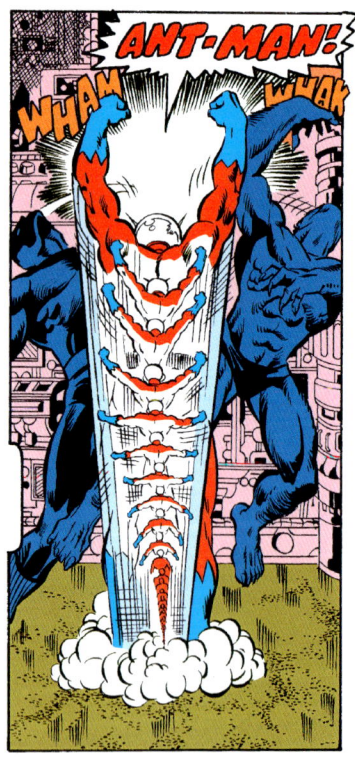

#47), and that idea went all the way to the movies. During his run Englehart, as always seeking soap-style drama, had depicted Pym's reaction to his wife being injured as a fury that touched on mania. Shooter enlarged on these hints of instability to show a revived Ultron playing with Pym's mind to the point of him finally forgetting the time since he joined the Avengers and attacking the current team as imposters. Hence some amazing Pérez art.

In Ultron's previous appearance that touched on his origins (Englehart had also used the robot out of context against the Inhumans), Ultron had declared himself to be the Vision's father. And he now referred to Pym as his own father. (The idea that the Vision's real parents could be said to be the two male figures whose components form him – Wonder Man and the Human Torch – isn't touched on here.) With the words 'Oedipus complex' uttered out loud, Ultron now wants to 'mate' with his mother, the Wasp, by transferring her mind into the body of an android of his creation (one whom he presumably doesn't think of as his daughter) called Jocasta (named after the mother and wife of Oedipus). This plan allows the story a frisson of horror without a full-on assault on the Comics Code and the Wasp. When Ultron returns for a second round during the Michael arc, and Wanda cracks his armour, he pleads for his 'mother' to save him. (When Ant-Man's insects swarm Wanda, she, with perhaps equal extremity, calls for her absent brother, Pietro.)

Pym eventually returns to normal between issues, next being seen, fully healthy, in *Marvel Team-Up* and swiftly returning to the Avengers, but this arc cemented the idea that Henry Pym was 'the mentally ill one', which led to him, in the 1980s, slapping Jan, and hence to divorce, attempts at redemption failing, and in recent years merging with Ultron into full-on villainy, Frankenstein as scientist and monster bonded together. When a version appears in Mark Millar's *Ultimates*, he's full-on abusive to Jan. This journey, from solid 1960s male authority figure to 2000s unhinged abuser, is an index of how distrustful creators and audience have become of what had been lurking behind the image of the steadfast, traditional husband. Shooter had been canny enough to fully engage with that process.

Attached to this saga was the complex business of Wonder Man having returned from the grave, and his mind being in some ways similar to that of the Vision. (Their 'brother' status was occasionally touched upon, but later on Wonder Man would pal up with the Beast in one of super hero comics' most long-lasting bromances.) The villain the Grim Reaper, Wonder Man's actual brother, whose motive had always been revenge for his brother's death, now had to resort to increasingly complicated reasons as to why he didn't just say 'oh, great' about his brother's revival. After the arc, Jocasta hung around, gaining Avenger status by default as she fought alongside the others against Michael.

One can only imagine how a family dinner involving Henry, Janet, Ultron, the Vision, Wonder Man, Jocasta and the Grim Reaper would go.

Shooter displays a great dichotomy when it comes to depicting women. At least three out of four of the major villains during his run are defeated because of a moment of weakness concerning a woman they care about. Graviton thinks that the woman who he's chosen as 'his' has chosen to die by suicide rather than be with him and thus destroys himself. Ultron runs when Iron Man bluffs that he'll destroy Jocasta. Michael kills himself when his lover Carina loses faith in his mission. (Nefaria just has the Vision drop on him from a great height, but not before we've heard about a new variation on the 'brought down by human weakness' angle: his age. Also, he shares Ultron's daddy issues, sealing his fate by killing his own 'creator': the professor who gave him his powers.) We can add to that the controlled Henry Pym being taken down by Jan turning on him and Ultron's defeat upon his second appearance starting with Jocasta rejecting him. Also, Shooter's villains almost always seek the forced 'companionship' of an unwilling woman. Carina has been set-up with Michael by her father(!), cosmic super villain the Collector, who wants her to learn all Michael's secrets then betray him, but instead she genuinely falls in love with the all-powerful man, to the point of accepting his decision to kill her father(!).

In the positive column, however, there's Shooter's clear enjoyment of Wanda's power, aided by Pérez's dynamic renditions of her using it. His Wanda goes so far as to say, in #166, that she's sick of Thor's overblown godhood and that Nefaria should beware of *her*, and the narrative celebrates rather than punishes her for knowing her value. Shooter significantly empowers her, making her the one threat (other than his 'human' weakness) that can defeat Ultron. (The image below was coloured by Shooter himself.)

Rather wonderfully, the only reason Wanda doesn't save the day single-handed on that occasion is that Captain America gets in the way. This happens again with Wonder Man yelling at Ms. Marvel to 'get to safety' in #172, despite the fact that she's just swatted the villain Tyrak with a lamp post. He thus gets himself zapped.

Shooter's Ms. Marvel (still with her own title when she starts appearing in *Avengers*) is enormously confident and competent. Her professional attitude and actions are the start of a new feeling for super hero comics, one that in later decades was to become the dominant mode in *Avengers*: the idea that heroes might not be talented amateurs, vaguely accepted by the authorities, but instead work procedurally and with responsibility, thinking like cops or soldiers. During the aforementioned Tyrak battle, Wonder Man thinks Carol is 'the most aggressive person' he's ever seen, that she doesn't just strike a pose and point like Wanda or Wasp, but 'hauls off and belts people… like a man would!' Clint, on the other hand, still having learned nothing, feels being punched out by Tyrak ought to take Carol down a peg. (In #175 he asks 'what do we need blondie for?' to which Moondragon points out that his superpower is shooting arrows.) Wonder Man's awkward willingness to listen earns Carol saying to him that a 'hunk like him might be worth educating'. Shooter's Wasp is also full of agency and charisma, trying desperately to look after Henry and establishing a life of her own, creating a fashion show in #167. She ends that issue, her launch having been ruined by a super villain battle, by telling the cheery Nighthawk to 'sit on it', though this was the year when *Happy Days*, where that snappy comeback originated, created the concept of 'jumping the shark'. Shooter gives Jan an exuberant, celebrity personality, with her often being the first one to introduce the group, and adding 'I'm the Wasp!' She also gets vastly increased powers (courtesy of that visit to *Marvel Team-Up* under writer Chris Claremont), now capable of knocking out a foe on her own with her sting. She says in #166 that only Henry gets away with treating her like a 'helpless woman', which says rather too much about the dynamics of their relationship.

Whether or not these arcs are sexist, they're certainly sexy. Previously the Vision and the Scarlet Witch lounging on a beach in swimming costumes had to serve as a metaphor for what they did on their honeymoon. Shooter, aided by Pérez, is considerably more daring. We glimpse a naked Jan and Henry embracing, and Ultron keeps Jan prisoner nude under two bands of metal. The Beast gets over a bout of ennui by finding that female fans find him attractive and is soon alluding to participating in threesomes. We listen in on Michael's psychic seduction of Carina – 'She feels his desire, senses-his offer' – and in #175, when they 'join, merging totally' for the first time, Michael 'softly slips between the delicate folds of Carina's soul'.

Along the way there are also some relatively subtle – and Comics Code dodging – moments like Jan in #170 looking down at her chest after mentioning how Henry likes her new costume and saying that makes four in favour of it.

The everyday people we meet in these pages continue a thread that unites all the 1970s *Avengers* writers: the use of crowd commentary to puncture any pomposity on the part of our heroes. They're also the source of some of Shooter's best dialogue. The workers who deliver Jocasta to the mansion in a crate in #170 'moved Neil Sedaka's pianer [*sic*] once' and interrupt Henry's reprise of events by telling him they're on a flat rate. Almost everyone who bothers our heroes in the street has a job-related question. The Avengers are now in a professional workplace and surrounded by working people. Shooter is the first writer to consider at any length what the official position of the team is. (Though it was touched on during the Kree/Skrull War.) He introduces Henry Peter Gyrich, an extraordinarily 1980s figure in his buzz cut and shades, with his catchphrase of 'I'm the government, mister!' This was at a time when Jimmy Carter was still the President. Reagan is clearly on the horizon. (According to writer Steven Grant in an interview, Gyrich was named after one of Shooter's cousins, and was supposed to be the grown-up version of Marvel children's character Peter the Little Pest.)

After some initial humiliation by Hawkeye, Gyrich sets rules and limits for the team, which they respond to by… learning to live with them like adults.

Across his arcs, Shooter has Captain America and Iron Man engage in a workplace dispute. Cap, perhaps unfairly, feels that Tony has been dropping the ball and, being preoccupied, not offering sufficient leadership. Cap starts giving orders in the field, and Tony feels the pressure of him undermining his authority. At one point, in #168, it looks like this sniping is going to escalate into a full-scale brawl when Cap punches Tony, but Wanda separates them, saying that the days of 'senseless brawling' between them are over. In the end, in #170, Cap comes to realize he was projecting his own reaction to losing his super-strength. Iron Man apologizes to him (and apologizes for Wanda too!). He offers to step down as chairman and even offers to reveal to Cap his secret identity, only for Cap to realize he has misjudged how seriously Iron Man takes the chairman's role. 'You lead… I'll follow—that's enough!', he says, and from then on actively supports Iron Man's decisions against the critique of others. It's a lovely bit of writing about a workplace relationship, and it's amazing – and very Shooter – that it's framed as a workplace chat rather than a super hero battle. (Though Pérez gives Cap a futuristic device to work out against during their chat, so it's not entirely a watercooler conversation.) When Shooter became Editor-in-Chief, he seems to have treated comics creators in the same way he treated these comics characters, expecting them to work within the system.

During Shooter's run, Jim Starlin (credited with 'other manual labour', with editor Archie Goodwin being the only other credit) uses *Avengers Annual #7* and *Marvel Two-in-One Annual #2* to finish the Warlock/Thanos cosmic saga he began in the pages of *Captain Marvel*. The Avengers are front and centre in their own *Annual*, not acknowledging their current plotlines but at the same time with the right line-up present and noting who's just popped in for this battle. It's a terrific piece of work, and I wonder if Starlin's 'gather every hero against one big threat' plot influenced Shooter's style on the regular title.

The Michael saga, or the Korvac saga as it has come to be known, after Michael's original villain identity, is wonderfully plotted, with Avengers being spirited away one by one (by the Collector, it turns out, in order to protect them from the cosmic being in hiding) as the team go about their usual business of fighting other villains. The Collector is betrayed by his daughter, Carina, who he's placed with Michael to watch him, allowing Michael to kill the villain. Starhawk, of the visiting Guardians of the Galaxy, alone senses Michael's presence and goes to confront him early (allowing us to hear Michael's origin story), only to have his memory and perception of the cosmic being erased. When the Avengers finally become aware of and locate Michael, the clue that gives away the fact that they're not just talking to an ordinary suburban guy is the fact that Starhawk can't see who they're talking to. It's a gorgeous moment of an enormously powerful being brought down by a tiny error. Battle ensues and our heroes (mostly) each get a moment to shine. (Captain America thumps Michael like he famously thumped Hitler, yelling that 'this is no god hitting you – no super-man! Just a man!') Wonder Man finds his courage and dies in battle, alongside, seemingly, many of his comrades. Michael realizes Carina has lost faith in him and lets himself perish. Carina attacks the Avengers, then destroys herself to join Michael. Moondragon tells Thor, the only other Avenger left standing, that Michael was a genuinely benevolent dictator who just wanted to fix the world. Before dying, he made sure that the heroes left scattered around the room will live.

And that was the end of Jim Shooter's *Avengers* run. He'd become Editor-in-Chief on the first working day of January 1978 and had held on to writing *Avengers* for a few more months, perhaps in order to complete his epic, before reluctantly giving up the book. (He'd had David Michelinie dialoguing over his plot in #173, #175 and #176, and Bill Mantlo in #174, but came back to script the ending himself. George Pérez had also been acknowledged as co-plotter here and there, which indicates he'd been providing more than the usual plot adjustments common to Marvel artists.)

Shooter, of all the writers we cover here, is the one that gets to end his time on the title on a deliberate high. He also gets to end it with the re-statement of his recurring thematic question, one he would later explore at length in the best-selling *Secret Wars* crossover event: is it possible to hold ultimate power and still be a good person?

It was a question that, as Editor-in-Chief, he might have considered often.

5

The Greatest Fill-In (1978)

Shooter's run on *Avengers* had included a couple of fill-in issues (#163's heavily disguised inventory story and #169's full-on departure from continuity), demonstrating that the departure of Englehart hadn't really solved the problem. Issue #178 spotlights the Beast (who was away guest-starring in other titles at the climax of the Michael saga) and doesn't continue from the previous issue, to the extent that one Danny Davids, in the lettercol of #182, asks 'what happened to all those Avengers who lay dying?' It also feels like a fill-in. But the difference is that this time it's placed as an interlude after the conclusion of an epic… and it's written by Steve Gerber.

Gerber (1947–2008) is arguably the greatest writer to work on a regular basis in the super hero universes of Marvel and DC. He was a little older than his peers, older than his new boss, Shooter, and everyone at Marvel seemed to know there was something special about him, something elevated. (He's named as 'resident psychoanalyst' when it's announced in #160 that Pérez is going to be co-plotting *Avengers*, and in #168 attributing the wrong issues in reference captions is referred to as 'the Gerber curse'.) He'd already had enormous success in turning muck monster the Man-Thing into an anthology about the everyday lives of those the creature encountered. He'd also turned his satirical creation *Howard the Duck* into an unlikely sales sensation. And he has quite the story to tell.

It's called 'The Martyr Perplex!' (The cover uneasily refers to it as 'Night of the Beast!', adds Cap and Wonder Man, and references the bar-room brawl, the visions of death and the presence of a super villain inside the covers as if in order to reassure the potential reader about what it refers to as 'the most off-beat *Avengers* epic ever!')

Howard wasn't Gerber's only philosopher hero. He'd established a put-upon, comedic sighing voice for monstrous Fantastic Four member The Thing in *Marvel Two-in-One*. So when we join the Beast in the 'singles scene' at a disco, we're not surprised that we immediately dive deep into intellectual Henry McCoy's psyche. But what he considers in this issue is a decade or more ahead of most super hero comics at the time. Having allowed himself to be thumped by an anti-mutant bigot and only fighting back when the man lays hands on others, Henry finds himself beset by the idea that the only woman he felt comfortable with at the club accepted him only because he's an Avenger. He's then accosted in the street by a vision of a wounded man who wears McCoy's injuries of the spirit. The apparition tells him that so much remains in him that needs killing. He knows that the Beast has questioned the 'wholesomeness' of his newfound acceptance by humans. He succumbs to the hero's own mental wounds and dies in front of him, only to be blasted into ash by a lightning bolt from the storm that rages around them.

The Beast runs for home. A caption says super heroes have a common coping tactic when the true danger is too horrible to contemplate: they contrive a physical peril as a distraction. Which adds a new dimension to a lot of previous *Avengers* infighting. Talking with a handful of his fellow Avengers, McCoy refers to his vision as a religious experience. A series of time dissolves gives the issue enormous space to breathe.

McCoy considers the agony he caused his parents by being a mutant and feels that, as an Avenger, he has come to see humanity as a mass, 'the world we're too busy saving to participate in'.

In the last seven pages, a super villain arrives: the Manipulator, who, it's revealed, has set the Beast up, in order to help a woman he went on a date with, to break into an apartment and steal a box. Opening that box will put him under the villain's control. Sure enough, Henry opens the box and is made docile, 'immobilized by the contents of his own mind'. The Manipulator demonstrates to some crime bosses that he can now control the Beast, leading to some amazing moments from Henry, his sung thoughts revealing that he hates the world. He changes the lyrics to 'Eleanor Rigby' to refer to his mentor Professor X as 'writing the words of a sermon that no one will–'. Then the villain mind-controls the criminals, too. He's visited by two government ('company') agents, who talk about how they're officially out of the mind-control business (perhaps a reference to the CIA's MK Ultra revelations?) but are pleased by this new option that doesn't use drugs. They're clearly impressed with the Manipulator's boast of being able to control any Avenger: 'One of them could turn against us someday.' They all exit the apartment.

The Beast, healed to some degree by his trip into his memories, comes to his senses and leaves. Then we see the government agents also ambushed by the apparition of the wounded man. That indicates one of two things: either the business of control in U.S. society is a series of boxes all inside each other and the agents are just as much victims as the Beast was… or religious experiences exist completely outside the doings of governments and super villains. (The Manipulator never quite says he was the one responsible for the Beast's initial vision.) What is it in the Beast that 'needed killing'? Is it his self-disgust at having accepted a distracting escape from anti-mutant bigotry? Is it his addiction to the systems of control and distraction that force him into a role? Is it his distance from the people he wants to help, created by the possibility of their prejudice? Or was the apparition that told him all that also part of the system? (Is it a gauche over-explanation or an apt continuation that in his only other appearance, in *Captain America*, the Manipulator is revealed, at the moment of his death, to be an android who is unaware of his own nature?)

As with all the best short stories, we're left to provide our own interpretation. Nothing is solved by the end, and there's only the tiniest nod toward redemption. This is Gerber considering how much control one can live with and how much one simply doesn't notice during the continuing narrative of a modern existence. And it appears at the end of Shooter's epic about how hard it is to be the one exerting the control. The artist is Carmine Infantino, who provides moody, emotive work reminiscent of Gene Colan's style on *Howard the Duck*. One of the government agents is named after new *Avengers* editor Roger Stern.

Avengers #178 is hard to recommend as a representative issue of the title, because it stands outside it and perhaps outside all super hero comics. It is, however, a masterpiece.

6

David Michelinie, Mark Gruenwald, Steven Grant… and Roger Stern (1978–1979)

David Michelinie was 30 years old when Jim Shooter picked him to first start putting dialogue to the finished art of his Michael epic, then to take over writing *Avengers*. He'd been part of an apprenticeship program at DC, during which he'd shaken up the status quo of Aquaman in an *Adventure Comics* run which saw the death of the hero's infant son. He'd also created sparky new characters like Claw the Unconquered, Gravedigger and the Star Hunters. It's easy to see what Shooter liked about his work. Michelinie was a professional, trained in the business, who had an edge of modernity and realism to his writing. (His most famous work lay ahead of him at this point. He would start writing *Iron Man* soon after he took on *Avengers* and be the first to depict Tony Stark as an alcoholic.) It was to be a while, however, before he properly got into his stride at *Avengers*. The rest of 1978 was mostly the work of others.

The excellent *Avengers Annual* #8, written by Roger Slifer, is a showcase of Pérez art and fun characterization, as Jan, irked that Hank is making her whole birthday (again, a little creepily) feel like a big event, is possessed by the gem of light-based villain Doctor Spectrum. (We're told she's vulnerable to being taken over because she has no 'obsessive desires', which is a welcome caveat considering we've recently seen how mentally tough the Wasp is.) Ms. Marvel gets to show off her powers in a fight in a gym, though notably she doesn't get to battle super-strong male Hyperion, but is provided with a female antagonist, the Amazon Thundra. The fight, wonderfully, is resolved by the Vision talking sense to Hyperion, and the reader is left feeling that more Slifer *Avengers* would be welcome.

In the regular title, however, there's yet another fill-in in #179 and #180, a two-parter by Tom DeFalco and Jim Mooney. It has now been three months since almost all the team were left apparently dead, and none of them have referred to it. This story has its moments (including the Beast referring to himself as a 'fabulous furry freak' – referencing the underground comic of that name – and the villain being motivated to break society's rules by the actions of President Nixon), but it ends with a bunch of ethical questions left awkwardly hanging and includes a weird scene of the Avengers voting about science vs. superstition. (Jan votes with Hank just because.) There's a line about the Avengers having to follow regulations when using Quinjets that just about ties it into current continuity, but this doesn't just feel like a fill-in, it feels like an *old* fill-in.

In #181, Micheline finally comes on-board, with a superstar artist: John Byrne. Byrne had previously pencilled an issue of Shooter's Nefaria storyline, but for the last year, he'd been drawing *X-Men*, and his partnership with Chris Claremont had accelerated that book's growth into one of Marvel's best-selling titles. If Pérez wasn't going to be drawing *Avengers* at this point, Byrne was his equal in terms of making the book feel modern, hi-tech and sparkly. The opening page, in a great artistic statement of newness, includes an actual still from the movie Wonder Man and the Beast are watching and establishes one of the tent poles of Michelinie's run: that these two are buddies who hang out together. (And them continuing to do so after Wonder Man leaves the team later on is both a mature character choice and an indication that, even if one is not a member, *Avengers* in this era will continue to check in with a wider cast of heroes.) The Beast vaguely continues one of his musings from the Gerber issue, about how super heroes live their lives for the public, bringing a bit of real, welcome meta-commentary into the main run of the book. Nobody mentions that time when they were all lying dead a few issues ago, but by this point it would be kind of weird if they did. Not only does nobody talk to themselves, there are only three thought bubbles in this busy issue; Michelinie's characters are usually talking *to* someone. There are also some lovely character moments. Michelinie retcons the messy decade of interactions between Wanda and Clint into a friendship. Clint says to her that he's being forced to leave at a time when 'you' (not emphasized in the text) might need him. Which leads to this lovely, and again not emphasized, response.

The issue is mainly devoted to Michelinie's big idea for the book: that Gyrich's government oversight of the team should be taken to its natural conclusion, with the authorities picking who should and should not be a member and reducing the rota to seven heroes. It's a smart conceit that creates character conflict, and it doesn't overstay its welcome. Guest writer Steven Grant's #190 finishes the plot, bringing things to a dramatic conclusion that restates the Avengers' purpose and freedom to act. (In that issue, Iron Man asks Gyrich if he's afraid his country will discover he exists, pre-dating the scandals of the 1980s with what the Beast in that issue calls 'Watergate refugees'.) Both the lettercols and the content of the comic during this period restate and reflect the idea that former members currently excluded from the team will continue to hang around and make guest appearances, which they start to do pretty much instantly. The cover to #181 (and a memorable splash page) depicts just how many people are these days gathered around the Avengers' meeting table. (Though the image cheats: it includes 23 characters, but only 15 of them have ever been Avengers.)

The smartest choice here is one that brings matters of race right back to the heart of the book. One of Gyrich's picks for membership is Black flying hero Sam Wilson, the Falcon. Never having been an Avenger and only having been seen at the Mansion on a couple of occasions, he's not even at the meeting. And look who gets the reaction shot when he's announced.

Hawkeye's main contribution to the drama of *Avengers* has always been him angrily leaving and merrily coming back, but this is the first time he's been *told* to leave. Gyrich cites government equal opportunities policy as one of the reasons behind his choice of a Black team member, noting that the Black Panther isn't available. Iron Man says that androids, mutants (and super heroes) are minorities too(!). Gyrich's apt picks include two mutants, two women and that android. With two shrinking heroes available, he picks the Wasp, leaving Hank out in the cold. (Neatly, the couple have a little loving scene of them negotiating that romantically, leaving any drama for the future.)

Wonderfully, the Falcon *doesn't appear in this issue or the next*. It's a very clever absence. Michelinie has chosen *exactly* the right character around which to centre this narrative. The Falcon is *of course* who Gyrich would pick. He's trusted and to some degree 'establishment', having been Cap's partner, and doesn't have the rebellious edge of other Black heroes. He's also, as Clint notes, underpowered ('That bozo's only powers are flying and rapping with birds!') and, as Iron Man adds, an untried relative stranger. He's also not there to speak for himself. He's being represented purely as a token. It becomes clear, when we finally see him in #183, that he hasn't even been asked whether or not he'd like to join. By the next issue he's ironically calling Gyrich 'massuh' and saying 'yassuh, I sho'be glad t'do that li'l thing.' On the one hand, it's a clever bit of digging at how representation initiatives can be Band-Aids that do nothing to deal with structural racism. On the other, one might ask how the readers would have responded if the Falcon had eagerly accepted the role, feeling it was about time he was offered Avengers membership. Because, honestly, it was. If the Falcon was meant to have been Captain America's equal partner all this time, why wasn't the idea of him being on Cap's team ever even mentioned? He's calling out affirmative action for being racist when the prior *lack* of that affirmative action has never been called out in the same way. We're asked to like him because he's reluctant to accept an honour that is actually only what he deserves.

Still, it works. Like him we do. Upon joining the team he first has to deal with Clint hanging around and telling him he isn't pulling his weight in fights, then with the more experienced members ordering him about on the battlefield.

He tries too hard to prove himself, rushing in, being captured and having to be rescued. There's a nice moment when he sees ex-Avenger Wonder Man in action and is downcast that he's the one having to stand in for such enormous power. Thor fails to notice him and nearly knocks him out of the sky. In #190 a government agent snaps at him, 'why, you dumb—!' At one point the Falcon refers to himself as being 'at the back of the bus' and notes that, when it comes to a decision about whether or not to answer a distress call in Soviet airspace, 'nobody thought to consult the token'. All in all, he becomes the reader point of view character: the newcomer we're cheering for. Which is, on the one hand, perhaps patronizing, but on the other, a majority white readership is being invited into a Black man's shoes (albeit by a white writer). Hawkeye gets solo adventures as we see what he's doing away from the team, but we're encouraged to see his continuing beef with the Falcon as wrong-headed, especially when Sam reaches out to Clint in #189 and Clint responds bitterly. We even see that Clint has a picture of Sam on his dartboard! (And a photo of Wanda on his wall.)

A solo story for the Falcon in *Marvel Premiere* is used as the springboard for him to gain new confidence, and soon after he's seen to successfully hold villains at bay until the others arrive – a proper team player. When it's time for Clint to be asked to re-join, in #192, Sam asks to be the one to call him.

This satisfying character arc is actually played out by a number of different writers, because, as the title of this chapter suggests, this phase of the comic is produced by many hands, their work held together and made to feel surprisingly unified by the editor throughout (except for the last two issues of the decade and the odd fill-in), Roger Stern. Stern is also a perennially under-appreciated comics writer, one of the unheralded greats of super hero comics, and I suspect he kept the tone of the book so uniform through many small interventions. On the edge of his thirties at the time, he'd featured the talents of the young John Byrne in his fanzine *C.P.L.* before ghosting some of Shooter's work at DC. He'd been an Assistant Editor at Marvel since 1977. Here was someone who knew all the players.

In #181–184, Michelinie sets up the new ongoing situation in the title and sends the Avengers into battle against Crusher Creel, the Absorbing Man, who mimics whatever he touches. But then he's asked to write the *Avengers* prose novel *The Man Who Stole Tomorrow* and gets time off to do so. So from #185 to #187, Mark Gruenwald and Steven Grant step in with something that's as far away from a fill-in as could be imagined: a saga about Wanda and Pietro's parentage that's at the heart of *Avengers* continuity. Issues #188–190 are put together by several different writers, but still feel unified and important, indicating that Stern has finally solved the perennial fill-in problem, and

Micheline returns to finish the decade with #191–193, in a run that would continue to #205.

Micheline's first arc seems very much like something his Marvel mentor Shooter would have written. The Absorbing Man feels he's misunderstood, and just wants to get away from the persecution of super heroes. Grabbing an everyday young woman, Sandy Herkowitz, for 'company', he makes his way to the docks, intending to board a ship for South America where, free from super heroes, he'll grab himself a banana republic to settle down in. The Avengers beat him through solid tactics, but there's also the feeling that he lets himself absorb the water around him and dissipates into it to maintain his dignity. Incredibly, Sandy wonders if it might have been okay to let him go. (In the lettercol of #189, Margaret O'Connell writes directly to Sandy, telling her that the people of banana republics need protecting too, and saying she shouldn't be condoning kidnapping and 'euphemistically-described … would-be rape'. To his credit, Michelinie replies, accepting that she's right and agreeing that it wouldn't have been acceptable to let Creel go.)

In the pages of *Iron Man*, through the character of Tony Stark's bodyguard and confidante, Bethany Cabe, Michelinie displays a verve for writing confident professional women who are at home in dangerous situations. In his *Avengers* issues we see some of that joy. 'Powee!' shouts Jan as she takes down an opponent with her newly powerful sting in #182. His thought bubbles for Wanda are full of capable, practical tactics and his Carol confidently gives battlefield orders. When a government agent puts a restraining hand on her arm in #183, she threatens him with a physical response. Michelinie's enjoyment of worldly, glamourous characters also results in panels like this…

Between Michelinie's arcs sits the tent pole of 1979's *Avengers*, the aforementioned 'Yesterday Quest', plotted by Mark Gruenwald and Steven Grant, with Michelinie providing dialogue. It aimed to finally clear up the morass of hints

and retcons concerning the parentage of Wanda and Pietro. I was lucky enough to correspond with Steven Grant about these issues, and he provided the following:

Prior to our involvement, Jim Shooter, during his stint writing *Avengers*, had started this 'true origin of Quicksilver and the Scarlet Witch' thread that was left dangling when he left the book to become Editor-in-Chief… There was regular pressure from fans to finish up that story. As happened with other things several times, David wasn't interested in that storyline, needed to take a sabbatical for a few months to write an *Avengers* prose novel. In any case, he, I would say with considerable justification, viewed the Wanda/Pietro history as a real rat's nest that would take considerable effort to unravel in any coherent way. Since Mark was a real continuity maven (far more than I was) Roger [Stern] thought Mark would be a good guy for sorting the story out, and at that point I was plot assisting Mark on things, so I was pulled into it.

Mark Gruenwald (1953–1996), 26 years old, was indeed the right person to sort this out, having been the editor of the fanzine *Omniverse*, which played the game of reconciling conflicting fictional texts into a single narrative, as if this were real world history and 'what really happened' could be established. He'd also contributed to DC's house magazine, *The Amazing World of DC Comics*. He'd been an Assistant Editor at Marvel for a year or so at this point. (Gruenwald died of a sudden heart attack, having continued to rise through the ranks at Marvel and become a beloved Bullpen lifer. As per his will, his ashes were mixed into the ink for the first printing of the trade paperback of his *Squadron Supreme* limited series.) Steven Grant, also 26, had been brought into Marvel by Stern, having worked on his fanzines. He had been suddenly asked, when crashing on Stern's sofa, to write an issue of *Marvel Two-in-One*, and, having been pleased by the pay check, moved to New York to try to get more comics gigs. He often worked with fellow fanzine veteran Gruenwald. (Grant was unlucky enough to share his name with one of the alter egos of Marvel character Moon Knight, leading some fans to think his was a pseudonym.)

Gruenwald and Grant assembled thirty pages of research into everything that had been established about Wanda and Pietro's family. One big element had been put in place by Byrne who, guesting in #166, had added to his art a few frames, not present in the script, of an old man with a locket containing pictures of Wanda and Pietro boarding a ship in Vladivostock, heading for the United States. (Exactly as Neal Adams had set up the whole Vision origin story with a single reaction shot, again unscripted.) Gruenwald and Grant decided that the old man was the siblings' first foster father, Django Maximoff, a Roma magician. Their mother, Magda, arrived heavily pregnant, fleeing their father, at Wundagore Mountain, the home of genetic meddler the High Evolutionary, where Bova, a genetically-engineered sentient cow(!), delivered them. Many precise retcons followed. The birth father who Magda was so afraid of was strongly hinted to be Magneto, the mutant super-villain who had brought Wanda and Pietro into his orbit when they first arrived in the United States.

The three issues that outline this resolved continuity (much of which still stands in 2025, though not the bit about Magneto) aren't a dry lecture but instead a gothic journey to self-knowledge with many magical battles along the way. They're a bit of a masterclass in how to satisfy both the geeky and drama-loving aspects of the fan psyche. But one aspect is worth commenting on in terms of the perception of female heroes at the time. In *Tales of Suspense* #72 Wanda had told Cap that she and Pietro were infants during the Second World War, which made sense for that issue, published in 1965, with Wanda then being in her early twenties. It would have still made sense in 1979, when Wanda and Pietro, both married and considering having families, would have been, appropriately, in their mid-thirties. And yet Gruenwald and Grant felt the need to retcon it, with Wanda having heard Django's stories about the war so often that she, incredibly, came to believe she'd been in it! It was, apparently, easier to believe that than to believe that these super heroes were 35. This was at a point before the establishment of Marvel's 'sliding timeline', in which all the events in the Marvel Universe since the creation of the Fantastic Four happened in the last fifteen years or so before the present day. In 1979, the FF's Ben Grimm was still seen as a Second World War veteran. So Wanda's de-aging might be the very first example of the old timescale starting to crack. 'To be honest', Grant told me, 'I don't think we ever thought about it... We just accepted the "Superman" premise of super hero comics, that the hero is always perpetually the same age. If that's really the first timeline slippage, let me know. I'd love to put that on my resume.'

After that, Jim Shooter plots and Bill Mantlo dialogues #188, a guest-written issue that takes the team into Soviet airspace to deal with some monsters. In the lettercol of the issue before, correspondent Bruce McCokindale had asked for more social relevance in the pages of the book, citing the work of Steve Gerber as the best example of what he was after. The reply was telling: that the problems of the 1960s and early 1970s were a lot easier to define – there wasn't a current Vietnam. But that uncertainty about current affairs actually had some positive results in that issue, in which the Soviets are portrayed with relative complexity, some as everyday people in need of help, some as ungrateful militaristic aggressors. Mantlo also wrote that year's *Annual* (#9), which was well-integrated into the current continuity, and presented the unlikely story of Tony Stark finding a robot designed by his father in the basement of Avengers Mansion. It turns out it's being controlled by a computer programmed with the personality of his mother, which could potentially have created another Oedipal AI Avengers family tree.

Steven Grant's #189 spotlighted Hawkeye outside the team, and demonstrated how, while so much had changed across the 1970s, some things remained exactly the same. 'Roger (Stern) suggested Deathbird for the villain', Grant told me. 'At that point she was just a mystery woman Chris [Claremont] kept using in *X-Men* and something about her drove Roger nuts, so he requested one thing: that when Hawkeye catches her, he gives her a big kiss. (Now that's the stuff of Me Too…) Just to tweak Chris… Guess that's what comes of suddenly becoming the most popular writer in the business.'

And that's just what happens. (A lettercol reply, presumably from new editor Jim Salicrup, in #193, calls Hawkeye 'an unconscious male chauvinist' and doesn't condone his actions, instead calling him 'a representative type'. It's interesting to note that these days Clint is one of the few heroes who has been allowed to age up, and now feels more like a Gen X type, a father figure to younger heroes who has changed with the times, but still has a touch of Old Guy about him.) In the same issue, Clint compares Deathbird to Moondragon, thinking that she's 'blasted superior' and, when he finds he's fighting an unknown flying assailant, assumes it's the Falcon!

When Michelinie returns to the book with #191, he firstly

finishes a plot Grant (with a plot credit by Stern) started in the issue before involving petrifying (literally) villain the Grey Gargoyle and then, in a final two-parter to close the decade, he does something rather special. With the aid of the Pittsburgh Comix Club, who are credited with a plot assist, he has the Avengers battle a new villain created by the industrial facilities in the city (his boss Jim Shooter's hometown), the geography of which the team explore. In his *Iron Man* run, Michelinie shows an interest in both the mechanisms of industry and in the lives of working people, and that's evident here. (Notably, when the Absorbing Man arrived at the docks, the longshoremen joined in with the Avengers' attack.) The villain, Inferno, is again misunderstood, but this time he turns out to be a tragic figure, a revenger of past injustice, so it's much more apt. He again, however, departs into the sea. The two-parter has guest artists Arvell Jones (one of the few Black artists in comics at the time) and Sal Buscema providing relatively rough pencils for now regular inker Dan Green.

The 1970s ends for *Avengers* with a caption promising that George Pérez will be back next issue. Across the entire decade, during which both the Avengers as a team and *Avengers* as a comic book had changed so hugely, the Scarlet Witch and the Wasp had become increasingly empowered, Black super heroes such as T'Challa and the Falcon had travelled from radical confrontation to affirmative action, an android and a mutant had found their 'mixed marriage' worked… and Hawkeye had learned precisely nothing. *Avengers* had invented the comics crossover event, changed the way heroes spoke to the audience, and suggested they might be professionals rather than amateurs. On several occasions it had put itself at the cutting edge of super hero comics, and influenced how they were told. Many of the plotlines that featured here (for instance, the personal journeys of Henry Pym, Wanda and the Vision) are still ongoing.

It's fascinating, and a little worrying, for me to look back and realize that this material shaped me as a person. Did this luxury dessert of a super hero comic contain some not-so-healthy ingredients? Sure. Did the wholesome outweigh the dubious? I think so. Does looking at the recipe allow one to gain more sustenance from what one has consumed? Perhaps.

I like to think, however, that what might be the central message of *Avengers* during the 1970s – that 'outsiders' of all kinds can and should be included in the ranks of the main, official, team – is one that supported me through those difficult years.

It's certainly a message that bears repeating today.

ACKNOWLEDGMENTS

I'd like to thank the following for their helpful notes and comments during the writing of this book. Any errors are, of course, my own.

Scott Edelman, Steven Grant, Simon Guerrier, Toby Hadoke, Lizbeth Myles, Jess Nevins, James Cooray Smith and Douglas Wolk.

ILLUSTRATIONS

ABOUT THE AUTHOR

Paul Cornell has written episodes of *Elementary*, *Doctor Who*, *Primeval*, *Robin Hood* and many other TV series. He has worked for every major comics company on series such as *I Walk With Monsters*, *The Modern Frankenstein*, *Saucer Country* and *This Damned Band*, as well as runs for Marvel and DC on *Batman and Robin*, *Wolverine* and *Young Avengers*. He is based in the UK.

MARVEL AGE OF COMICS

Explore the series!

www.bloomsbury.com/marvel-books

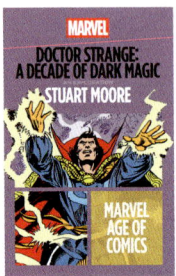

Doctor Strange: A Decade of Dark Magic
by **Stuart Moore**

The story of one of Marvel's most bizarre, otherworldly heroes, beginning with his creation at the hands of Stan Lee and artist/plotter Steve Ditko, and discussed against the backdrop of one of the most turbulent decades in American history.

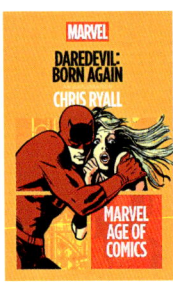

Daredevil: Born Again
by **Chris Ryall**

A smart, meticulous look into the compelling and original storyline of *Daredevil: Born Again*, its gorgeous and unique artwork, and its overall influence in the decades since its release.

Spider-Man: Miles Morales
by **Ytasha L. Womack**

A look at the hugely successful reimagining of one of the most popular super hero characters of all time.